D1484743

The Other Feud

William Anderson "Devil Anse" Hatfield in the Civil War

Philip Hatfield, PhD.

Foreword by
James M. Prichard

For President Jimmy Carter
c/o Karen DiPietro – Best regards,
It's an Honor Sir –

Revised Fourth Edition, 2021

35th Star Publishing
Charleston, West Virginia
www.35thstar.com

Fourth edition, 2021.
Printed in the United States of America.

ISBN-13: 978-1-7350739-6-5
ISBN-10: 1-7350739-6-2
Library of Congress Control Number: 2021937102

35th Star Publishing
Charleston, West Virginia
www.35thstar.com

On the cover: Devil Anse Hatfield images courtesy of the West Virginia State Archives, Charleston, West Virginia; 45th Battalion Virginia Infantry flag courtesy of the American Civil War Museum, Richmond, Virginia.

Cover design by Studio 6th Sense LLC

Publisher's Cataloging-in-Publication Data

Names: Hatfield, Philip, author.
Title: The Other Feud: William Anderson "Devil Anse" Hatfield in the Civil War / Philip Hatfield
Description: Fourth edition. | Charleston, West Virginia : 35th Star Publishing, 2021. | Includes bibliographic references and index.
Identifiers: LCCN 2021937102 | ISBN 978-1-7350739-6-5.
Subjects: BISAC: HISTORY / United States / Civil War Period (1850-1877) | HISTORY / United States / State & Local / South (AL, AR, FL, GA, KY, LA, MS, NC, SC, TN, VA, WV)

William Anderson "Devil Anse" Hatfield.
Author's Collection.

To the memory of my parents,
who instilled within me
a lifelong love of history.

Calvin Lee Hatfield
Freda Jane Hatfield

Contents

Illustrations, Maps, Photographs

Foreword

Since the publication of the late Michael Feldman's *Inside War* over forty years ago, historians have increasingly focused their attention on guerrilla warfare during the Civil War. Daniel E. Sutherland's *A Savage Conflict* (2006) provided a comprehensive overview of the role of guerrillas throughout the conflict, yet little has been written about the brutal guerrilla warfare in the mountainous region that marked the border between Kentucky, Virginia and West Virginia. To date the primary works remain John David Preston's *The Civil War in the Big Sandy Valley of Kentucky* (2008) and Dr. Brian McKnight's *Contested Borderland: The Civil War in Appalachian Kentucky and Virginia* (2006).

The regions' rugged terrain made large scale military operations virtually impossible. By 1863 the border remained a "No Man's Land" between the Union and Confederate lines that witnessed savage small scale fighting. It is no coincidence that the same region would be plagued by post-war violence, including the legendary Hatfield-McCoy Feud of the 1880's.

In this work Dr. Philip Hatfield provides an in-depth study of the

Confederate service of the post war feud chieftain, William Anderson "Devil Anse" Hatfield. Following his brief service as a young officer in the regular army, Hatfield emerged as an active participant in the guerrilla warfare that plagued the Kentucky-Virginia border. The isolated killings, ambushes and raids he participated in became his education in violence. The summary execution of local Unionist prisoners he participated in during the conflict would be repeated with the vigilante executions of the three McCoy brothers in 1882.

Dr. Hatfield dispels many of the longstanding myths and misrepresentations about the legendary feudist's wartime exploits and provides a well-researched glimpse of wartime conditions in the mountainous region. In this respect alone, *The Other Feud* is a valuable contribution to the study of the Civil War in the Big Sandy Valley.

Dr. Hatfield's work also sheds further light on the legendary Hatfield-McCoy Feud. In her highly respected study, *Feud: Hatfields, McCoys and Social Change in Appalachia, 1860-1900* (1988), Dr. Altina L. Waller found no connection between wartime events and the outbreak of violence between the two mountain clans. Hatfield's research calls for a serious reconsideration of Dr. Waller's conclusions. This work will be appreciated by both those interested in the Civil War in the Appalachians as well as the feud era.

James M. Prichard
Historian, Independent Researcher

Introduction

Numerous books are written about the famous Hatfield and McCoy feud, although most shroud the story with myths and folklore. Regardless, this feud was very real and very bloody, claiming the lives of more than twelve men between 1878 and 1891 in the mountainous Tug River Valley region of southeastern West Virginia and Kentucky. Details of the complex story behind the Hatfield and McCoy feud are beyond the scope of this study, but a little-known fact is that most of the men involved in the feud were also Civil War veterans. One of them was the iconic Hatfield patriarch, William Anderson "Devil Anse" Hatfield, whose military career, like the feud, is often enmeshed in myth and misinformation. As a result, many published accounts of Hatfield's Confederate service are inaccurate.

Although none of Devil Anse's immediate family had slaves, nor any direct economic ties to the institution, the Hatfield family for the most part aligned with the Confederacy; however, some of the extended family and friends also served in the Union Army. Similarly, while the McCoy family was largely aligned with the South, they too had members serving in Union regiments and home guard companies. Only a few McCoys served in the same unit as Devil Anse Hatfield and later sided with him in the feud.[1] (See Appendix Tables 1 and 2)

In one feud account, the writer reports that Randall McCoy and Devil Anse fought together in a late war guerrilla company known as the "Logan Wildcats." However, there is no reliable evidence supporting that story beyond family tradition. Other accounts posit they were together on various partisan raids during 1864-1865, although many of those versions are also based solely on family tradition.[2]

While details of Randall McCoy's service are minimal in extant military records, there is evidence that he was held in a Union prison from July 6, 1863, through July 7, 1865. His capture and incarceration are discussed later in this work, although another popular version asserts that McCoy never served in the Civil War at all.

Given the many variations published of the feudists' military service, it is not surprising that many scholars now believe sectionalist tensions were not a primary cause of the feud.[3] Traditionally, historians agreed that feud tensions emerged during the Civil War; however, modern authors seeking to dismiss the notion typically argue that economic factors during the Reconstruction period and mixed sectional alliances in both the Hatfield and McCoy families negate the idea. Yet, many events transpired during the Civil War involving the later feudists, their extended families and friends indicating there was a more complex, multi-factorial causative sequence deeply rooted in sectionalist division. Thus, the Civil War "...remains a major factor in understanding Devil Anse and the feud."[4]

Several popular feud sources correctly indicate that the wartime experiences of the feudists and their families were generally quite polarized and malevolent, although many historic inaccuracies within those works make it difficult to rely on their conclusions. Similarly, rebuttals to the notion of sectional alliances playing a casual role in feud violence are often problematic because their accounts of the feudists Civil War service frequently conflict with data found in military service records.[5]

Another point to consider is that the Hatfield and McCoy families were not the only clans who experienced inter-familial violence during the Reconstruction era. According to John E. Pearce in his book, *Days of Darkness: The Feuds of Eastern Kentucky*, there were many similar "feuds" occurring in the region during the Reconstruction era, with nearly all having roots in sectionalist tensions from the Civil War. While Pearce acknowledges many accounts were drawn from family tradition which is always suspect for implicit bias, there is also more reliable evidence from various court records showing several altercations, robberies and murders occurring during the Civil War and in the Reconstruction period were associated with later interfamilial conflicts, i.e. "feuds." The contextual implication for the present study is that there was an enduring and embittered legacy from the Civil War present for many years afterward in the mountain culture in both West Virginia and Kentucky.[6]

Further, there is a large body of modern behavioral science research spanning several decades demonstrating the complex psychological effects of combat among veterans. Those data consistently show that most combat veterans suffer chronic impairments in their familial and social relationships as a result of their wartime experiences. In that context, attempting to separate the effects of the feudists' wartime experiences from later life seems unrealistic despite recent attempts to minimize the role of the Civil War in later feud violence.[7]

Therefore, the purpose of this study is to review the evidence of Devil Anse's military service and distinguish between facts and myths found in most traditionally accepted accounts in context of the question of what role the Civil War played in later feud violence.

William Anderson Hatfield was born on September 9, 1839, in Logan County, Virginia (now West Virginia), in the Mate's Creek area. He was the son of Ephraim Hatfield (b. 1811) and Nancy Vance. From his youth until the Civil War, Devil Anse worked as a farmer.[8]

Devil Anse was a leader even from childhood and held the respect of all who knew him. He was also recognized in the Tug River Valley region as a crack marksman and expert horseman. Although questionable, the nickname "Devil Anse" is said to have originated from a peculiar childhood habit of catching and training bear cubs as pets.[9]

Even before the Civil War, his precocious and strong personality made Devil Anse an obvious leader. While probably apocryphal, one story suggests that the youthful Hatfield once single-handedly wrestled and subdued a catamount, a cat similar to a mountain lion. His mother is even supposed to have said, "He isn't afraid of the Devil himself."[10]

Devil Anse married his long-time sweetheart, Levicy Chafin, on April 18, 1861, just a few days after the attack on Fort Sumter escalated the already hostile tensions across the nation into a Civil War. Chafin was the daughter of a neighboring farmer, and they eventually had thirteen children together. Only three of their eight sons later became feudists, however.[11]

Hatfield Feudists.
West Virginia State Archives.

Area of Operations
West Virginia, Kentucky,
Southwestern Virginia
1862–1864
Scale in miles
0
10
Ohio River
OHIO
WEST VIRGINIA
KENTUCKY
VIRGINIA
TENNESSEE
Calhoun
Jackson
Point Pleasant
Mason
Putnam
Winfield
Kanawha
Clay
Greenup
Cattletsburg
Guyandotte
Boyd
N
Coals Mouth
Charleston
Wayne C.H.
Cabell
Great Kanawha River
Fayette
Wayne
Boone
Louisa
Lawrence
Tug River
Guyandotte River
Boone C.H.
Fayette C.H.
Logan C.H.
Johnson
Raleigh
Paintsville
Martin
Raleigh C.H.
Logan
Williamson
Wyoming
Pond Creek
Pineville
Flat Top Mtn.
Floyd
Pike
Pikeville
Knott
McDowell
Mercer
Buchanan
Letcher
Dickenson
Tazwell
Tazwell
Bland
Wise
Russell
Wythe
Lebanon
Smyth
Wytheville
Saltville
Virginia & Tennessee RR
Abingdon
Scott
Washington
South Fork Holston River
Bristol
Grayson
Independence
George Skoch

1
1861: Militia Service

The first year of the Civil War was one of the more ambiguous eras of Devil Anse Hatfield's life. All white males from ages eighteen to forty-five in Virginia were required to serve in a militia company during the antebellum period; Devil Anse was no exception, although various writers have suggested he was in no less than three different military organizations during 1861. Unfortunately, most offer only anecdotal accounts based on family tradition without supporting documentation from military or other records. This chapter reviews the most common versions of Hatfield's military affiliations in 1861 and available evidence (or lack thereof) for each.[12]

A widely accepted description of Hatfield's early war service is that he served in the 129th Regiment, Virginia Militia. Although his name is not found on any related documents, regimental muster rolls from the 129th Regiment reveal many of Hatfield's family members and neighbors were in those organizations early in the Civil War. In addition, records of the 187th Regiment Virginia Militia from nearby Boone and Wayne Counties also contain the names of several of his family and friends, but Devil Anse is not found among them.[13]

While it is not unreasonable to infer that Devil Anse would have served in one of those two regiments because his family members and friends did, one writer recently expressed doubt that Hatfield saw any service in the militia or otherwise until 1862. However, that author also acknowledges the 129th Regiment had several men present in small skirmishes and battles who are not found on muster rolls.[14]

Incomplete militia records were not uncommon in western Virginia. Many such organizations failed to keep records, or if they did, neglected to turn them into the state despite the Virginia Code of 1858 requiring men to enroll their names with the local tax collectors. Company officers were also required to submit annual reports of their membership to the state Adjutant General; however, many of those documents were lost or destroyed in the war. For example, when the Logan County courthouse was burned by Federal troops in February 1862, the fire destroyed most, if not all, of the county records. Another problem was that a significant number of men in western Virginia refused to sign muster rolls for fear of being identified and bringing retaliation upon their families. Many were also afraid that placing their names on muster rolls made them vulnerable to being drafted into the regular armies and forced to serve far from their home areas leaving their families vulnerable to harm from enemy forces.[15]

Another potential reason Devil Anse does not appear on 1861 militia rolls was that he had recently married his sweetheart, Levicy Chafin, on April 18, 1861, just a few days after the attack on Fort Sumter at Charleston, South Carolina. It seems likely that he would not have wanted to risk leaving her alone with growing sectionalist hostilities in the region and potentially being taken away into some other theatre of the war, although this is speculative. Alternatively, since hundreds of other men placed their names on the rolls despite similar risks, these factors may not fully account for incomplete muster rolls. This may be particularly true since those who did not sign the rolls could not receive pay, because the government would have no record of their enlistment.[16]

Coleman Hatfield, a Hatfield biographer, wrote in his book, *Tale of the Devil,* that Devil Anse served in an antebellum era volunteer company known as the "Logan Wildcats." Other authors have similarly claimed Devil Anse was in the Logan Wildcats during the Civil War, including one who claimed he did so after deserting the regular army. The Logan Wildcats originally organized as a volunteer company in 1858, although a company logbook containing muster rolls from 1858-1860 fails to show Devil Anse as a member. In 1861, many new volunteers joined the company, and they mustered into Confederate service under command of Captain James M. Lawson as Company D, 36th Virginia Infantry on May 27, 1861. Devil Anse's name does not appear on any of that regiment's muster rolls or service records, however. Note also that some authors have suggested there were two different companies using that nickname, but the antebellum volunteer company was simply an earlier incarnation of the 1861 organization.[17]

Coleman Hatfield also cited a journal kept by the regimental clerk of the 129th Regiment Virginia Militia as evidence that he belonged to an antebellum militia company in that regiment. The biographer wrote, "In the journal which was kept for the company by Dr. Joseph Hinchman, Hatfield was allotted a certain area on the Tug Fork of Sandy River, all of the soldiers within the allotted area being led by Hatfield as their captain. The remainder of the county was then divided up in like manner so that each 'captain' had a parcel of the territory and all soldiers in training were led by the respective 'captains' from the various areas of the entire county. They trained at regular intervals in those days."[18]

The journal cited initially belonged to Ulysses S. Hinchman's nephew, James Henry Hinchman of Logan County, but he was not a physician. Rather, Ulysses S. Hinchman was a physician and farmer according to the 1860 U.S. Census. Captain James H. Hinchman served as clerk of the 129th Regiment Virginia Militia from November 3, 1852 through September 10, 1858. Then, Captain Ulysses S. Hinchman served as the regimental clerk through 1860. Like many antebellum militia organizations in western Virginia, the 129th Regiment had several Union supporters in the ranks and was divided when the war began; then, Captain James H. Hinchman and the other Unionists left the 129th Regiment and formed a home guard company. In January 1862, Captain Hinchman was ordered to "force march" his company to Camp Russell, Virginia, even if he had to "march them day and night."[19]

An article published in the November 3, 1936 *Logan Telegraph* (written over forty years after the feud) contains excerpts from the Hinchman's journal, describing it as "…a painstakingly kept record" of the regiment's activities and identifies several members, although it does not mention Devil Anse. However, the article also erroneously states James F. Hinchman was the original clerk; the only James F. Hinchman found in the 1860 U.S. Census is Ulysses Hinchman's eleven-year-old son. A later article in the *Logan Banner* of August 13, 1995 also mentions the Hinchman's journal, but similarly makes no mention of Devil Anse Hatfield.[20]

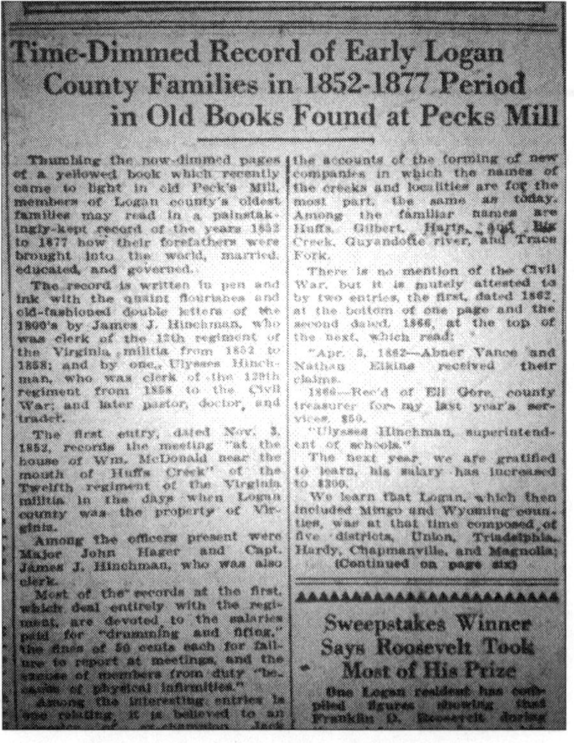

Time-Dimmed Record of Early Logan County Families in 1852-1877 Period in Old Books Found at Pecks Mill

Thumbing the now-dimmed pages of a yellowed book which recently came to light in old Peck's Mill, members of Logan county's oldest families may read in a painstakingly-kept record of the years 1852 to 1877 how their forefathers were brought into the world, married, educated, and governed.

The record is written in pen and ink with the quaint flourishes and old-fashioned double letters of the 1800's by James J. Hinchman, who was clerk of the 12th regiment of the Virginia militia from 1852 to 1858; and by one, Ulysses Hinchman, who was clerk of the 129th regiment from 1858 to the Civil War; and later pastor, doctor, and trader.

The first entry, dated Nov. 3, 1852, records the meeting "at the house of Wm. McDonald near the mouth of Huffs Creek" of the Twelfth regiment of the Virginia militia in the days when Logan county was the property of Virginia.

Among the officers present were Major John Hager and Capt. James J. Hinchman, who was also clerk.

Most of the records at the first, which deal entirely with the regiment, are devoted to the salaries paid for "drumming and fifing," the fines of 50 cents each for failure to report at meetings, and the excuse of members from duty "because of physical infirmities."

Among the interesting entries is one relating, it is believed to an [illegible]

the accounts of the forming of new companies in which the names of the creeks and localities are for the most part, the same as today. Among the familiar names are Huffs, Gilbert, Harts, and Big Creek, Guyandotte river, and Trace Fork.

There is no mention of the Civil War, but it is mutely attested to by two entries, the first, dated 1862, at the bottom of one page and the second dated, 1866, at the top of the next, which read:

"Apr. 5, 1862—Abner Vance and Nathan Elkins received their claims.

1866—Rec'd of Eli Gore, county treasurer for my last year's services, $50.

"Ulysses Hinchman, superintendent of schools."

The next year, we are gratified to learn, his salary has increased to $200.

We learn that Logan, which then included Mingo and Wyoming counties, was at that time composed of five districts, Union, Triadelphia, Hardy, Chapmanville, and Magnolia;

(Continued on page six)

Sweepstakes Winner Says Roosevelt Took Most of His Prize

One Logan resident has compiled figures showing that Franklin D. Roosevelt during [illegible]

Logan Telegraph, November 3, 1936.
Courtesy of Brandon R. Kirk.

Note that Coleman Hatfield's book, *Tale of the Devil,* is a collection of anecdotal and family tradition accounts, rather than an archival evidence-based narrative. Yet, it seems doubtful that the biographer confabulated the story knowing the Hinchman family members could easily contradict any inaccuracies. Nonetheless, it is concerning that newspaper reports written four decades or more after the feud citing the Hinchman's journal also fail to mention Hatfield's name as a member of the antebellum 129th Regiment Virginia Militia. By that time, Devil Anse was a national icon and the reporter would have likely mentioned him. Further, Hinchman family descendants could not confirm that Devil Anse is mentioned in the journal. Thus, we are left with Coleman Hatfield's testimony that the journal shows the feudist was a member of the antebellum 129th Regiment Virginia Militia. On the other hand, given what is known of his character, it is unlikely Devil Anse would have stayed home when his family and friends were going off to fight in the 129th Regiment during the early months of the war.[21]

The 129th and 187th regiments belonged to the 27th Brigade of Virginia state militia under Brigadier General Alfred Beckley. In 1861, six companies of the 129th Regiment hailed from Logan and Nicholas Counties, while the smaller 187th Regiment was comprised of only two companies from Boone County. The regiment was commanded by Colonel John Dejarnott, and his vice-commander was Lieutenant Colonel William A. Dempsey.[22]

The company officers were as follows:

Captain Lorenzo D. Chambers' Company (No. 1): 1st Lieutenant George Avis; 2nd Lieutenant Andrew S. Bryan; and 2nd Lieutenant Christian Patterson. Most of this company transferred into Company No. 4 when Lieutenant Avis was promoted to Captain.[23]

Captain George Avis's Company (No. 4): 1st Lieutenant James E. Perry; 2nd Lieutenant James R. Chambers; and 2nd Lieutenant John Justice. In addition, Captain Bennett Carter's Company: 1st Lieutenant Enos Adkins; 2nd Lieutenant Edward Garrett; and 2nd Lieutenant Issac G. Gaston. Carter's Company was later re-organized into Company B, 34th Battalion Virginia Cavalry.[24]

Captain David Wilkinson's Company (No. 8): 1st Lieutenant

William Baisden; 2nd Lieutenant John S. Baisden; and 2nd Lieutenant James Mead, Sr. Lieutenant William Baisden was promoted to captain on September 3, 1861, and he formed a new company. At that time, James Mead, Sr., was promoted to 1st Lieutenant; John S. Baisden was promoted to 2nd Lieutenant, and Sergeant John R. McCoy was promoted to 2nd Lieutenant. Twenty-eight privates also transferred into Captain Baisden's Company.[25]

Captain Thomas Buchanan's Company: 1st Lieutenant James M. White and 2nd Lieutenant Joseph Skaggs. This company divided in 1861 when the war began as many members including Buchanan were Union supporters. Buchanan later became a 2nd Lieutenant in the 4th West Virginia Cavalry in 1864. In March 1865, he obtained authorization from Governor Arthur I. Boreman to recruit a Union home guard company. However, as the Logan area was strongly pro-Southern, Buchanan groused that he could receive no help from the Union army in recruiting because he was then located seventy miles inside of Confederate lines.[26]

Thomas Buchanan's brother John, however, was Southern leaning and organized a new company from the remnant of the former militia company that became part of the 129th Regiment in 1861. This instance is a good example of how sectionalist tensions often divided families in western Virginia during the Civil War; it is unknown whether they reconciled after the conflict ended. Devil Anse and John Buchanan were neighbors until April 1861 when Hatfield married Levicy Chafin and moved out of his parents' home; he later served under Buchanan in both the Virginia State Line and 45th Battalion Virginia Infantry. Hence, it is very likely that Hatfield was also a member of John Buchanan's 1861 militia company.[27]

In another source, the writer reported that the 129th Regiment also had a company formed in 1861 at Guyandotte with sixty-six men, captained by Thomas Thornburg, and that another was organized in October 1861 at Wyoming County by Captain William Walker, but Devil Anse was not mentioned. However, 129th Regiment Virginia Militia records do not show either Walker or Thornburg on the muster rolls.[28]

The first entry in James H. Hinchman's journal of the 129th Regiment Virginia Militia was on November 3, 1852; he recorded that a meeting was held "at the house of Wm. McDonald near the mouth of Huffs Creek" on that date. Among those present were Major John Hager, Calvary Hatfield and Reece Browning. The antebellum era version of the 129th Regiment also had field music, (fifes and drums) and musicians were paid two dollars per day for performing during drill and ceremonies. Members who missed a mandatory drill or meeting were fined fifty cents, unless they could produce an excuse for "physical infirmities."[29]

For three days service during regular musters, officers were paid ten dollars. When the 12th Regiment re-organized as the 129th Regiment in September 1858, James Hinchman's successor was his uncle, Captain Ulysses S. Hinchman of Logan, who continued the journal as the 129th Regiment Virginia Militia through 1860. At a meeting of officers on September 10, 1858, John Dejarnott was elected colonel; and K. McComas, first major; Reece Browning, second major; and Ulysses Hinchman, captain and regimental clerk.[30]

Officers in attendance were Captains George Avis, James H. Hinchman, John Starr, John Hatfield, John Chapman, and Barnabus Carter; and Lieutenants Martin Doss, George Bryant, Granville Riffe, Louis White, Charles Staton and Green A. Clark. After 1861, there are only minimal entries mentioning the Civil War, one being a later note that the Logan County Sheriff had "failed to settle his taxes" in 1861.[31]

During the antebellum period, Logan County included the area now known as Mingo County, as well as what is now Wyoming County. The state militia therein covered five districts: Union, Triadelphia, Hardy, Chapmanville, and Magnolia. By late 1860, there were also new companies forming at Huffs, Gilbert, Harts and Big Creek, and along the Guyandotte River, and Trace Fork. The old 12th Regiment had at least seven companies prior to 1858, spread across those areas.[32]

Each company was commanded by a captain who was responsible for a specific parcel of the territory; all training activities in the district were then organized by the respective captains under the overall command of the regimental commander, a colonel, and his staff.

According to Coleman Hatfield's account, Devil Anse's antebellum era company was responsible for the areas located along the Tug Fork of the Sandy River. Family oral tradition holds that Devil Anse was in command of all militia troops in that area, but there is no record of such, or that he was ever in command of any organization larger than a company during the war.[33]

According to Captain Ulysses S. Hinchman, the 129th Regiment "...trained at regular intervals at Logan Court House" during the pre-war years in accordance with state law. This is of interest, as contemporaneous sources reflect that the typical antebellum militia muster days were usually no more than a picnic, and many ended in a drunken brawl. For example, Major Michael Egan commanded a battalion of Virginia state militia from 1857-1861 in western Virginia; he described a typical muster day: "...the boys after drill would usually indulge in a little horse trading, or swapping, talk of, and appoint log-rolling, rail-maulings, house-raisings, apple-cuttings, corn-huskings, and many other kinds of frolics..." As the state was trying to reorganize the militia, a correspondent to the *Weekly Register* in Mason County quipped, "With the inauguration of the new order of things generally, let us for Heaven's sake, have some improvement upon these nonsensical farces known as militia musters."[34]

Another example was the volunteer militia company known as the "Kanawha Rifles" in Kanawha County, which formed in 1859. One young private in that outfit remarked how muster days usually had little to do with military matters. The militiaman described spending muster days in full dress uniform, sporting his rifle on his shoulder, marching back and forth while "...proudly guarding the fried chicken and lemonade." Such accounts contrast with information found in Captain Ulysses Hinchman's journal; according to his record, the 129th Regiment maintained a high level of discipline and regular drill during the antebellum period, and as war became imminent in late 1860, they intensified frequency of musters for training.[35]

Devil Anse's Side of the Story

Several years after the war during the feud era, Hatfield was brought to Charleston by United States Marshalls on November 21, 1889 on charges of selling liquor without paying the required tax; i.e. "boot legging." Ultimately, the charges against Hatfield were revealed in court to be the result of a conspiracy by law officers who planned to return him to Kentucky for the $1,500 bounty.[36]

As he awaited trial, the November 23, 1889 *Wheeling Intelligencer* interviewed Devil Anse. In a two-hour conversation, Hatfield gave a brief account of his military service, "I served in the militia in 1861, and regularly enlisted in 1862 in the Confederate army, as First Lieutenant in the Forty-Fifth [Battalion] Virginia Infantry. I resigned in 1863, and then recruited a company which was kept in service in Wayne, Cabell, and other border counties of West Virginia and Kentucky."[37]

Notice that Devil Anse did not specifically state to which militia regiment he belonged in 1861, and as earlier noted, muster rolls from the 129th and 187th Regiments Virginia Militia do not contain his name. On the other hand, several Hatfield family members later recalled having fought alongside Devil Anse in the 129th militia early in the war, although most such accounts originated years after the feud.[38]

Summarily, while admittedly inconclusive, a review of available evidence suggests that Devil Anse served with the 129th Regiment in 1861; however, future research may show otherwise. Both the 129th and 187th Virginia Militia Regiments were active in western Virginia during the early months of the Civil War and were involved in a skirmish at Wayne Court House in August 1861.[39]

On August 25-26, 1861, at Wayne Court House, elements of the 129th, 167th, and 187th Regiments Virginia Militia attempted to defend the town from Union troops but were unsuccessful and tensions piqued. At nearby Ceredo, the 5th [West] Virginia Volunteer Infantry (Union) was forming, and a local volunteer company known as the Fairview Rifle Guards had recently left the area to join the Confederate army, leaving residents unprotected.[40]

Devil Anse

TELLS THE TRUE HISTORY

Of the Famous Hatfield-McCoy Feud to an Intelligencer Representative,

And Puts His Mark to the Statement When Read to Him.

A VERY THRILLING RECITAL.

The Famous Head of the Hatfield Family Not So Black as Painted

By Sensational Reporters—How Marshal White Got His Consent to go to Charleston—A Conspiracy by Kentucky Detectives Frustrated by the Court.

Wheeling Intelligencer, November 23, 1889. Library of Congress.

Skirmish at Wayne Court House

The 167th Regiment Virginia Militia was from Wayne County, and following a recent rout during a skirmish in Cabell County, by late August 1861, many residents were concerned they did not have a will to fight. The citizens had good reason to be concerned; Wayne County had a reputation for being violently pro-Southern, and quickly became a focus of Union forces. The *Catlettsburg Advocate* noted "perhaps nowhere in western Virginia has there been a viler nest of Secessionists than at Wayne Court House."[41]

The local militiamen still willing to defend the town devised a plan to do so despite the doubting citizens, however. One source indicated "Rebel forces had reportedly been 'fortifying themselves' in the courthouse at Trout's Hill for about a month." Militia leaders determined that when word came that Union troops were approaching, a man would ring the courthouse bell calling for them to rush to the courthouse under arms and take action.[42]

On the evening of August 25, 1861, a detachment of fifty-four soldiers from the 5th [West] Virginia Infantry at Ceredo marched into town and went to the Court House on Trout's Hill. Their immediate goal was to capture the town for the Union by breaking up the Southern militia encamped there, as well as to capture county records while "holding up the stars and stripes in the face of the bushwhackers," according to one Union officer.[43]

Once they entered Wayne Court House, one of the Union soldiers rang the bell, not knowing it was the signal for the militia to rush to the courthouse with muskets. In a few minutes, a small group of about twelve militiamen showed up and exchanged gunfire with the Union detachment at the town square. Heavily outnumbered, one of the militiamen was killed, and eight were captured by Federals.[44]

The Union detachment quickly sent for help, and two more companies of 100 to 150 men (sources vary) from Ceredo arrived August 26, 1861. The Confederates also received reinforcements from the 129th and 187th Regiments Virginia Militia from Boone and Logan Counties. Heavy skirmishing continued and pitched at 5:00 PM when the militia attempted to retake the town.[45]

After a few minutes of "thick and fast" gunfire from the Union soldiers, the Southern militia were once again forced to retreat. A resident who was then just seven years old later recalled, "For two days the families were kept shut up in their homes, and when the bullets whistled too viciously, the mother would have the children lie flat on the floor to escape any stray balls that might enter a window."[46]

An unidentified Union soldier of the 5th [West] Virginia Infantry who participated sent an account to the *Ironton Register*, published on August 29, 1861:

> The rebels suspected more men had been sent for and determined to prevent their reaching the hill...When we came in sight, they gathered together and commenced firing upon us...found the fire in our faces and the fire in the rear...rather hot. I was not long in dismounting and making a trial of the Enfield rifle I had with me. But on the third volley of our men, the rebels fled into the woods.
>
> Some of them had good guns, and all the squad that attacked us, (supposed to be sixty or eighty) were strangers in this part of the country. They came from Cabell or Logan County. It is believed that of the whole force that surrounded our men on the hill, about one hundred were drilled men who had seen service.[47]

The 5th [West] Virginia soldier continued:

> In the skirmish we had two of our men were slightly wounded...We have no means of ascertaining accurately the loss of the enemy. There is no doubt that they lost six or eight killed and three wounded, two badly and one slightly. Our loss in the whole affair was three prisoners and one of our new rifles.[48]

On August 28, 1861, the Federals left Wayne Court House under the cover of darkness. Accounts from locals and the *New York Times* offered quite different versions of the circumstances associated with the Federal exodus. Locals claimed the Union forces found the militia planned to blockade the road between Trout's Hill and Ceredo with fallen trees, and in lieu of having to fight their way out, the Unionists eloped under cover of darkness. The militia then declared a victory, thinking they had driven the Union troops off. In contrast, the *New York Times* account indicated that the Federals had no further reason to stay, having accomplished their main objective and captured the county records, so they simply left town.[49]

Fight at Boone Court House

During the last week of August 1861, Union commanders at Charleston learned of a contingent of Confederate militia posted at Boone County Court House. Colonel James V. Guthrie, who commanded the Union garrison at Charleston, received orders from Brigadier General Jacob D. Cox to organize a detachment comprised of Company G (Captain Samuel C. Rook) and Company K, (Captain William H. Squires) of the 26th Ohio Volunteer Infantry, under command of Lieutenant Colonel David A. Enyart.[50]

The detachment also included Company A, 1st Kentucky Infantry under Captain Joseph T. Wheeler; and Companies B and D of the 4th West Virginia Infantry under Captains John L. Vance and Arza M. Goodspeed, respectively, along with Captain Seth J. Simmonds' Battery of the 1st Kentucky Light Artillery. Their objective was to "beat up" the Confederates, a force of roughly 150 men, comprised of the 129th and 187th Regiments Virginia Militia under Colonel Ezekiel Miller. Some Confederate partisans masquerading as Union men at General Cox's camp learned of the pending movement and sent word to Colonel Miller.[51]

The Federal detachment of 550 troops left Charleston on two government steamers, arriving at Brownstown (modern Marmet, West Virginia) on August 30, 1861. Disembarking, they marched through mountainous terrain to the village of Peytona, where two companies of home guards joined the detachment with another 200 men. Some accounts state the home guards had no commanding officer, but the men had recently elected Francis Mathers and John Spurlock as captains of the respective companies; however, neither were yet formally commissioned. As such, Lieutenant Colonel Enyart placed the home guards under the immediate authority of Captain Joseph T. Wheeler, Company A, 1st Kentucky, who in turn placed them under a Corporal in his company.[52]

The two 4th West Virginia companies were not present during this affair, as they were left at Peytona with orders to scout the area as the rear guard. A letter to the *Gallipolis Journal* of September 12, 1861, supposedly written by Colonel Guthrie, indicated that Captain Wheeler's company (1st Kentucky Infantry) and Captain Rook's company (26th Ohio Volunteer Infantry) along with the Peytona Home Guards were engaged at Boone Court House. Another news organ, the *Cleveland Morning Leader*, similarly reported on September 6, 1861 that the 4th West Virginia companies were held in reserve at Peytona, so that the main Federal force "...might fall back upon it, if they found the enemy too strong."[53]

Also, neither General Cox's official correspondence nor his later memoirs mention the 4th West Virginia as battle participants. The 26th Ohio regimental history simply doesn't mention them at all. One author recently opined that they "seemingly remained at Peytona...guarding the Federal rear and route of the retreat as a blocking force, should the expedition to Boone Court House go awry." However, in other official correspondence, General Jacob Cox indicated it was two companies of the 1st Kentucky Infantry and a company of home guards were who attacked the Confederate militia.[54]

Colonel Ezekiel Miller soon learned of the Federal advance and sent some of the militia out to meet the Federals, intending to strike first before they surrounded Boone Court House. They clashed on August 31 at Red House (modern Danville, West Virginia), and after a twenty-minute "desperate" skirmish, the Confederates lost one killed, two wounded, and six captured, along with several horses and rifles, and there were no Union casualties. Afterward, the militia returned to

Boone Court House and residents anxiously hid in the hills around the village.[55]

The Federal detachment arrived on Knob Hill above Boone Court House on September 1, 1861. Lieutenant Colonel Enyart's plan was for the Peytona Home Guards to advance southward along the Logan-Boone road, attempting to draw fire without yet initiating an open engagement. If it worked, they were to fall back to Knob Hill, and join a flank attack on the Confederate right with Company A, 1st Kentucky Infantry and the 26th Ohio Volunteer Infantry. Captain Wheeler directed the Corporal in charge of the home guards to anchor their left flank along the South bank of the Little Coal River. Shortly after stepping off, the home guards opened fire as they advanced.[56]

The Confederates promptly returned a heavy fire, and it soon appeared that Lieutenant Colonel Enyart's plan was working. However, instead of turning back to support the planned flank movement as ordered, the home guards "defiantly" continued to advance, refusing to fall back because it was their first opportunity to fight the "overbearing secessionists."This frustrated the Federal opportunity for a consolidated flank movement. Meanwhile, Companies A and G of the 26th Ohio Volunteer Infantry began their advance down the hill, with cover fire from two guns of Simmonds' Battery.[57]

Moving at the double quick, they swept down the slope "like an avalanche" towards the militia, firing and yelling as they ran. The rattle of heavy musketry and smoke filled the valley as fighting pitched when they neared Confederate lines. As Captain Wheeler's Company A and the Peytona Home Guards simultaneously clamped down on the Southerner's left, the militiamen stubbornly stood their ground. General Cox described the Federal advance as "rapid and vigorous." Then, after roughly thirty minutes of fighting, being outnumbered and employing outdated muskets, the militia's lines disintegrated into a chaotic retreat. In the process, the Boone Court House and several houses were burned.[58]

The Southern contingent placed blame for the fires upon the Federals, while General Cox reported, "In the fight the village was burned. I have no particulars as to how or by whom." In a later

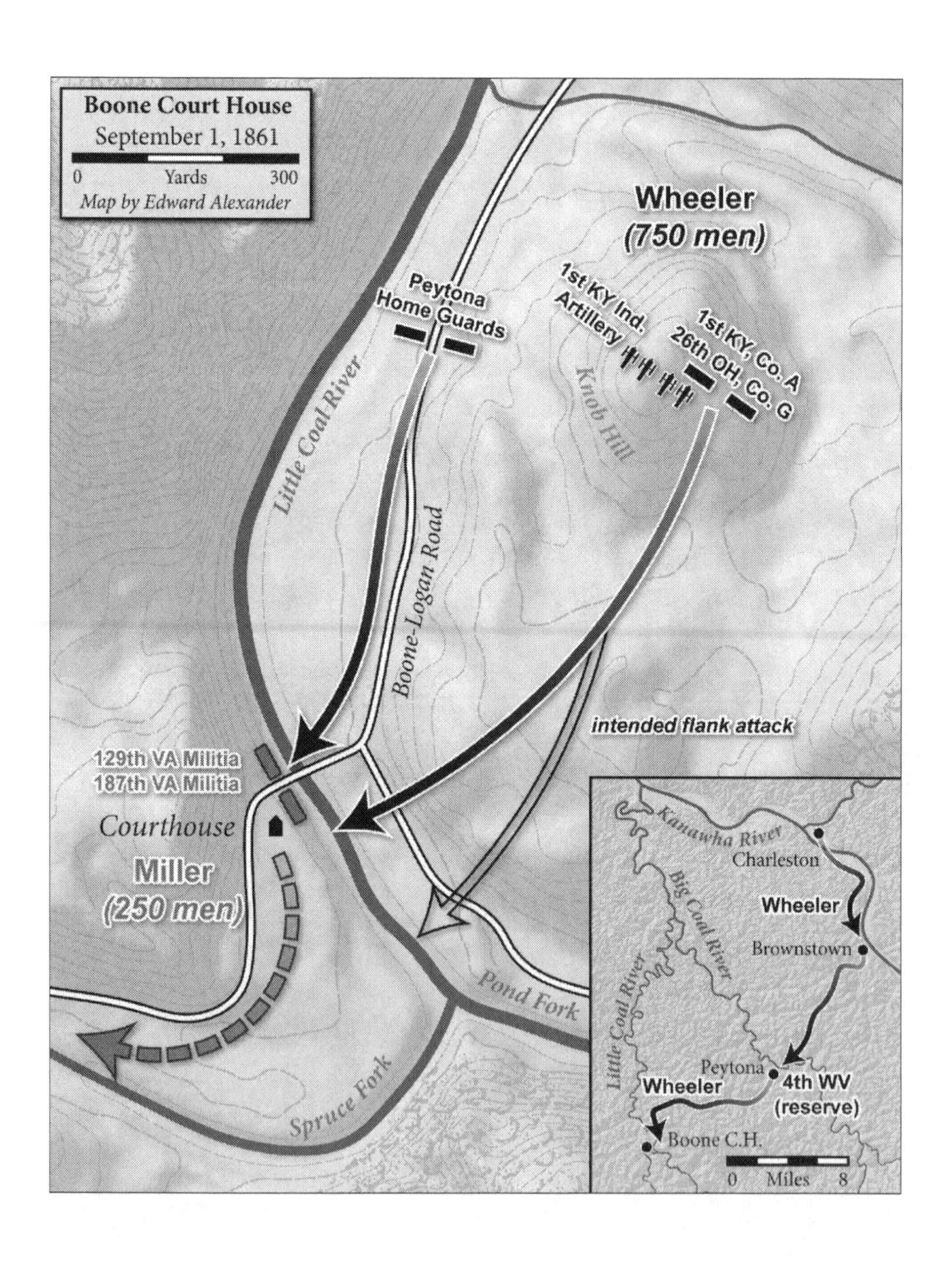
Boone Court House
September 1, 1861
0 Yards 300
Map by Edward Alexander
Wheeler
(750 men)
Peytona
Home Guards
1st KY Ind.
Artillery
1st KY, Co. A
26th OH, Co. G
Knob Hill
Little Coal River
Boone-Logan Road
intended flank attack
129th VA Militia
187th VA Militia
Courthouse
Miller
(250 men)
Pond Fork
Spruce Fork
Kanawha River
Charleston
Wheeler
Brownstown
Big Coal River
Little Coal River
Peytona
Wheeler
4th WV
(reserve)
Boone C.H.
0 Miles 8

communication with General William S. Rosecrans, however, General Cox wrote that it was two companies of the 1st Kentucky and a company of home guards who set some houses ablaze, explaining that was done because the Confederate militia "retreated into them and were using them as fortifications." Cox also took a moment to qualify the comment with "I have severely reprobated every such act, and nothing but extreme necessity can sanction it."[59]

Afterward, Federal and Confederate casualty accounts as well as troop strengths were quite discrepant. General Cox reported that six Federals were wounded; he also wrote that the Union troops counted twenty-five Confederates killed, noting also "it is supposed there are more." Another account claimed approximately thirty-five Southern militiamen were killed, and five were captured. The Union loss was cited as none killed, and six wounded according to the *Ironton Register*. However, when Colonel Ezekiel Miller's account of the battle was passed through military channels, one officer later wrote there were forty-two Union prisoners of war taken from the "miscreant band" who burned the courthouse and were being shipped off to a Richmond prison.[60]

Colonel John Dejarnott, 129th Regiment Virginia Militia, also wrote of the action, "Commanded by myself...on the 1st of Sept Boone CH [Court House] was burnt and the forces from Logan killed and wounded 61 of the Federals, and only two of our men taken prisoner, none killed."[61]

The *Richmond Daily Dispatch* also mentioned the fighting at Boone Court House as follows, "Boone county Court-House, near which the fight occurred on Sunday last, and which was subsequently burned by the Federal troops..."

The *Gallipolis Journal*, a pro-Union organ, reported the following:

> Thirty-five of their number are known to be killed, and five taken prisoners. The loss on our side was none killed and six wounded. Corporal Nolan [James W. Nowlen, Company A, 1st Kentucky] received a severe but not fatal wound in the breast. A private who was carrying a small Union flag, was fired at from a house as the

> troops were marching through the town, the ball passing through both legs.
>
> This so fired the soldiers that they concluded to fire the town, which was accordingly done, and an hour later the village of Boone was among the things that were, every house in it, including the courthouse and jail, being burned to the ground. Among the things captured are twenty-two horses and a considerable quantity of arms, consisting of flint-lock muskets, double-barrel shotguns, and rifles.[62]

The *Gallipolis Journal* correspondent also mentioned an unusual event during the Civil War:

> On the return of the troops they were met at a place called Peytona, twelve miles north of Boone, by a party of ladies, who had formed themselves into a company of Union Home Guards. The boys lent them their muskets, and they were put through the facings by one of the officers, who speaks very highly of their proficiency in drill. The boys, after giving nine hearty cheers for the patriotic ladies of Peytona, took up their line of march for Charleston, and are now on board this boat, together with the prisoners, wounded and contrabands, on their way to camp.[63]

After the fight at Boone Court House, tensions in the region escalated. Colonel John Dejarnott, 129th Regiment, took 225 men, and once more marched from Logan Court House, Virginia, to Boone Court House, roughly twenty-five miles away on September 15, 1861. There, they planned to "repel an invasion by the Federal forces but Colonel Dejarnott indicated, "they failed to show at that [place]."[64]

Battle at Kanawha Gap

The 129th Regiment Virginia Militia next saw action on September 25, 1861, at Kanawha Gap near modern Chapmanville, West Virginia. Captain William Baisden, who commanded a company of the 129th Regiment, certified "on honor" that he and his men had a "Fight at Chapmanville 25 September - our forces was 225 men, Federal forces 700, killed 60 lost two."[65]

Union military records are minimal for details of the action at Kanawha Gap, although several newspapers contained varying accounts of the battle. The *Cincinnati Commercial* reported on October 3, 1861 that the Federals were said to have "surrounded and attacked the rebels at Chapmansville, and after a short engagement completely routed them..." Another newspaper in Washington, D.C., the *National Republican*, overstated the battle results would "...restore permanent peace to the Virginia counties western of the Kanawha..."[66]

A soldier in the 34th Ohio Volunteer Infantry, aka "Piatt's Zouaves," published a letter to the editor in the *Chicago Daily Tribune* on October 9, 1861; The Zouave correspondent wrote:

> ...Their force was 450 infantry and 50 cavalry. Our force was 560...After marching 42 miles, they came upon the enemy, who were behind breastworks, but could not stand our boys' steady fire, for they retreated in utter consternation, their Col. J.W. Davis, of Greenbrier, Va, (but the traitor is a native of Portsmouth, Ohio,) being mortally wounded...[we] took a secesh flag, 20 feet long with FIFTEEN STARS, 4 horses, 1 wagon, 10 rifles (one of which I claim), 12 muskets, and commissary stores.
>
> The route of the enemy was complete...They fled the moment their commander fell. The fight lasted about 10 minutes opposite the breastworks, but a running fire was kept up previous to that, by the Bushwhackers and rebel cavalry for two hours...we came suddenly upon their breastworks, immediately in line of our

entire column.

It was made on the side of a knoll, between two mountain sides, the road running between the mountain on our left…a force of 100 men on the mountain top on our right, who raked our column from the front to the center…Our men naturally fired upon the rebels on their right, steadily advancing up the road, until within 20 feet of the enemy's works, when the rebels suddenly opened fire, from their right, left and center.

The order…to flank right and left was immediately responded to by the Zouaves with a hurrah, a Zouave yell, and a cry of "wood up" from Little Red; a dash by our boys upon the enemy's breastworks, above which about 300 rebel heads suddenly appeared, unknown by our men till that moment. They sent a perfect storm of bullets around, over, under, and into our men. A few minutes more and our boys were inside the breastworks, chasing them over the mountains, the enemy running away like cowards as they proved to be...[67]

Another soldier in the 34th Ohio sent the editors of the *Bucyrus Journal* his account:

…our force all told was between five and six hundred…We jumped to our feet, got into our places right faced, and were off on the double quick, in less time than it takes to write it. Every few minutes the fire was repeated, and so on for the distance of three miles, when they commenced firing on us from different parts of the hill. We kept on until the fire became so hot that the Colonel ordered skirmishers out on the right, when we again moved on up the hill, until we came up to what is called the Kanawa [Kanawha] Gap.

Right above this place they had erected an ambush breastwork upon which they could sweep the road for one hundred yards.

> They had placed their Cavalry on the road to draw us into this place, where they supposed they could whip us and cut us up at will; but before entering this place, more skirmishers were thrown out, and we advanced without knowing anything about their designs and before we were aware of it, they poured in a volley, which made the very mountains tremble, but not so with the Zouaves - they were as firm as the rock of Gibraltar.
>
> We returned their fire, when the command was given to charge bayonets, which was done with a wild and a hearty "Zouave." We carried their breastworks at the point of the bayonet, at which they retreated, not being able to withstand our old muskets and rusty bayonets. Off they went, as though Satan, with all the imps of the infernal regions, was after them...We remained in Chapmansville that night and the following day. About four o'clock it commenced raining, and at two o'clock we were called out to start for home on account of being out of provisions. We started amid rain and mud, and marched all day without a mouthful to eat until four o'clock in the afternoon, by which time we were at Cole [Coal] River...Several of the boys and myself went into a field, and brought out a lot of pumpkins, which we held up over the fire, in slices, of which we poor, half famished boys made a meal, and I acknowledge, we relished it.[68]

After the battle, a flurry of discrepant casualty reports flooded the media. For example, the *Cleveland Morning Leader* reported that the Union force killed "between fifty and sixty" and Federals losing only four killed and eight wounded. Another news organ, the Washington D.C. based *Evening Star*, indicated the Confederates lost sixty killed and "seventy prisoners." Meanwhile, the *National Republican* reported "...the enemy [Confederates] lost one hundred killed and a proportionate number of wounded..." According to the *Chicago Tribune*, the Union "...killed 20, took 3 prisoners...They left 29 dead behind...We lost 3 killed, 9 wounded, one since died."[69]

The *Bucyrus Journal* also reported Federal casualties as four killed and nine wounded…their loss are estimated at thirty killed, and a large number of wounded. This is the report of some of their own men." In contrast, a pro-Southern paper, the *Staunton Spectator* reported the Confederates had only eighty troops engaged at Kanawha Gap, and that Federal losses were forty killed and "a number wounded" with the Confederate militia losing just two killed and "three or four slightly wounded."[70]

After the battle at Kanawha Gap, the 129th Regiment Virginia Militia returned to Logan. Colonel Dejarnott next recorded that the 129th Regiment marched to the mouth of Pigeon [Creek] along the Sandy River, on October 25, 1861. Covering a distance of twenty-two miles, their intent was again to "repel the Union forces" although the colonel stated they were "not able to find them." On November 10, 1861, Lieutenant Colonel William A. Dempsey later wrote that he marched with 100 men to Twelve Pole, in Logan County, "to repel an invasion by the Union men - killed 7 & 2 wounded." Thus ended 1861 for the 129th Regiment Virginia Militia.[71]

Historical marker for the Battle of Kanawha Gap, at the Chapmanville exit of Route 119. West Virginia Division of Culture and History.

Soldiers of the 34th Ohio Volunteer Infantry Regiment, Piatt's Zouaves. Library of Congress.

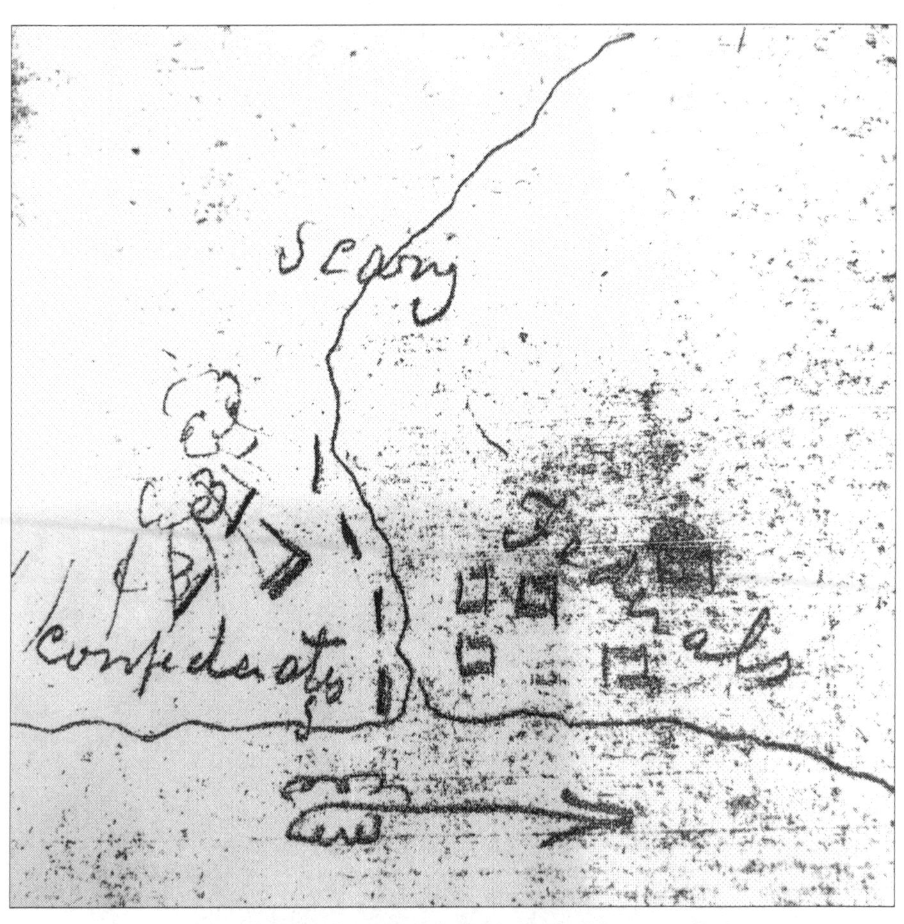

Map of Scary Creek battlefield sketched by a resident of the area immediately after the battle. The arrow indicates the Kanawha River. West Virginia State Archives.

The Devil at Scary Creek

Another popular but mythical story originating in Hatfield family tradition also places Devil Anse with yet another outfit, the Sandy Rangers from Wayne County, under Captain James Corns. This company fought at the July 18, 1861, battle of Scary Creek in Putnam County. There, Union forces under Colonel Carr B. White, comprised of the 12th Ohio Volunteer Infantry, and one company of the 21st Ohio Volunteer Infantry engaged Confederates under Brigadier General Henry A. Wise, a former governor of Virginia, in a sanguine fight lasting nearly twelve hours.[72]

Late in the day, the Federal infantry advanced near the wooden bridge spanning Scary Creek, a tributary of the Kanawha River. Crossing would allow them to make a direct and frontal assault on the Confederate position. Posted nearby at the base of Coal Mountain were the Sandy Rangers, who were also nicknamed the "Blood Tubs" because many of the men wore bright red hunting caps and red flannel shirts. That company later became part of the 8th Virginia Cavalry in August 1861.[73]

As it became clear that the Federals were about to breach their lines, the Sandy Rangers galloped toward the bridge, and Captain Corns led them in a fierce countercharge, driving the Federals back while singing a ballad known as "Bullets and Steel." Devil Anse is said to have been riding with the Sandy Rangers. While Captain Corn's dramatic countercharge is documented, Hatfield's presence is not. Incidentally, William S. "Rebel Bill" Smith of Wayne County was present with the Sandy Rangers at Scary Creek as a member of a local volunteer company known as the "Fairview Rifles."[74]

Note also that the Sandy Rangers were later attached to the 36th Virginia Infantry for a period before becoming part of the 8th Virginia Cavalry in 1862. This may be another reason that inaccurate accounts emerged placing Devil Anse not only at Scary Creek, but also in the Logan Wildcats, who became Company D of the 36th Virginia.[75]

Logan Wildcats Myth

As earlier discussed, a commonly accepted, but inaccurate, version of Devil Anse's military service in 1861 is the notion that he served in a company known as the Logan Wildcats in 1861. The antebellum era volunteer company by that name mustered into the 36th Virginia Infantry as Company D in May 1861, although Hatfield's name does not appear on their muster rolls.[76]

One author asserted that Devil Anse and Randall McCoy were both "leaders of a Confederate guerrilla unit, the Logan Wildcats..." which has no basis in military records. Similarly, another writer mentions that Devil Anse, his brothers Ellison and Elias, as well as their father, Ephraim, enlisted in a company of the Virginia State Line which was led by former officers of the Logan Wildcats, and that Devil Anse had been a member of the latter. There is only family tradition supporting that notion, however. Historian Otis Rice wrote that Hatfield's uncle, Jim Vance, was said to have threatened Asa Harmon McCoy, Randall McCoy's brother by saying the Logan Wildcats would "pay him a visit." McCoy had recently returned home after discharge from the army in December 1864, and was murdered in February 1865; however, Rice did not mention Devil Anse as a member of the Logan Wildcats.[77]

Coleman Hatfield also wrote that the journal kept by Joseph and Ulysses Hinchman for the 12th and 129th Regiments of Virginia Militia indicated Devil Anse was captain of a company known as the Logan Wildcats before the Civil War; however, as noted earlier, a log book from that company fails to show Devil Anse's name. Also, two newspaper articles in the *Logan Banner* listing names of the 12th and 129th Militia officers and members did not mention the Logan Wildcats or Hatfield. Given the feudists fame, it seems likely the reporters would have mentioned him.[78]

Coleman Hatfield's version of the story begins with an article from the May 14, 1861 *Kanawha Valley Star* of a ceremony occurring on May 11, 1861 at Chapmanville when the new volunteers raised a Confederate national flag. The writer described how dozens of young men and women waxed patriotic listening to several hours of intense oratory motivating males to enlist, including Devil Anse, although his presence is otherwise undocumented.[79]

Two weeks later, at a similar ceremony held in Logan, where the Logan Wildcats were organized, Devil Anse is said to have been "...caught up in the excitement and climbed on one of the wagons that rolled out of Logan, taking the men to Charleston, where they would be mustered into the regiment organized by John McCausland, an erstwhile instructor at Virginia Military Institute who had been ordered by Robert E. Lee to begin training troops for the struggle."[80]

Keep in mind, however, that Devil Anse made no mention of serving in the Logan Wildcats, before or during the war, nor did he mention serving in the 36th Virginia Infantry in 1861-1862 in his 1889 description of military service published in an interview with the *Wheeling Intelligencer*. To the contrary, Devil Anse stated only that he served in the "militia" during the first year of the war. As regimental muster rolls and other service documents show no evidence that he was in Company D, 36th Virginia Infantry, a.k.a. the "Logan Wildcats," it is apocryphal.[81]

Coleman Hatfield's narrative goes on to include an account from Devil Anse's mother, Nancy Hatfield, regarding an incident that supposedly wounded his pride, and had more to do with his enlistment than anything else. The patriarch's mother also mentioned he was the captain of a militia company before the war, although we cannot be certain of the accuracy.[82]

Nancy Hatfield's account as cited by Coleman Hatfield is as follows:

> My boy Ansie, was captain of all the soldiers from Beech to Mate. When the war was about to start, they were practicing being solders among the homeguards on the other side over in Kentucky, and Ansie and two other neighbor boys, Mose Chafin and Davie Mounts, went over to watch them march where General Bill France had men on Peter Creek. General Bill said our boys were spies. When Virginia seceded, General Bill said to Ansie, 'Look at the shape your state is in.'

> He made one of his men fight Ansie, and my boy got the best of him. Then he set another man on Ansie, and my boy then downed the second man. Then General Bill told his company to drive our boys back across the river into Virginia. They threw rocks at Ansie and Mose and Davie. They had to run to keep from being killed, because General Bill had fifty men or more. This caused a whole lot of trouble because all of the boys on our side of the river were terribly mad at the way General Bill's soldiers had treated them.[83]

Coleman Hatfield further indicated that one of the men Francis chose to fight Devil Anse was Asa Harmon McCoy, Randall McCoy's brother, who was murdered in 1865. While likely apocryphal, this account would explain much of the tensions between Hatfield and Randall, if proven. Note that Captain William Francis, Jr., a.k.a. "General Bill" of Peter Creek in Pike County, Kentucky, was not a general officer of the militia or regular forces; rather, he led a Union home guard company, and "general" was no more than a local nickname. Other sources note locals also often referred to William Francis as "Yankee Bill." Francis was killed in 1863, supposedly by Devil Anse, although that is based on oral tradition.[84]

Summarily, several anecdotal family and oral tradition based accounts exist, suggesting that Devil Anse served in three different military organizations in 1861: the 129th Regiment Virginia Militia, the Sandy Rangers at the July 18, 1861 battle at Scary Creek, who later became Company K of the 8th Virginia Cavalry, and also in the "Logan Wildcats," who became Company D, 36th Virginia Infantry. However, the most reliable version of his early war service places him with the 129th Regiment Virginia Militia in 1861, rather than the others.

Ultimately, the uncertainty surrounding Devil Anse's military career does not end in 1861. On March 7, 1862, the Virginia Militia underwent a major overhaul in preparation for the Confederate Conscription Act (the draft), and men along the Tug River Valley began enlisting in a new organization that was known as the Virginia State Line. While Hatfield's service in that organization is well documented, there are still several unanswered questions and inaccurate accounts of his activities in 1862-1863.

THE LOGAN WILD CATS' BATTLE FLAG.

"The Flag That Never Was Captured."

Compliments of FRANK C. DUDLEY, Editor of The Logan Democrat.
At the Chapmanville Reunion Tuesday May 7, 1907.

Logan Banner, April 24, 1914. Holding the flag on the left is Henry Clay Ragland who in 1888 founded the Logan Banner newspaper. The flag was made by the wives and sweethearts of men from Peach Creek.

Logan Wildcats, (Company C, 36th Virginia Infantry) 1900 Reunion. Courtesy Harlan Justice. Devil Anse is present in this image. Second from left is Ed Garrett. Sitting is Alex Burton and behind him is Uncle Dyke Garrett, On Dyke's left is Henry Clay Ragland.

Reverse side of photo: (not in order) 1. "Uncle Bill" Wm. Lucas. 2. "Uncle Ed" Edward Garrett 3. Alexander Burton 4. "Uncle Dyke" Wm. Garrett 5. James Henderson. 6. Capt. Hugh Avis 7. Sgt. James Dingess. 8. Wm. "Bill" Duty 9. Fulton Ferrell 10. Capt. Asyntax McDonald "Uncle Styne" 11. Lorenzo Stollings 12. Gnoch Baker 13. Reuben White 14. James Allen 15. Maj. Henry C. Ragland 16. Floyd Barker 17. Scott McDonald 18. Benjamin Spencer 19. Hamilton McDonald 20. Boliver McDonald. 21. Jas. W. "Buncre Jim" Blevins. 22. ___ Belcher 23. George Hale 24. Hugh Butcher (Not a Vet) 25. Calhoun Chapman.

2

1862: Virginia State Line

One of the better documented eras of Devil Anse Hatfield's military service was in mid-1862, when he received a commission as 1st Lieutenant of Cavalry in the Virginia State Line (VSL). There is no evidence found in military records that he ever served in a cavalry unit however, as the VSL regiment he belonged to was infantry.[85]

The VSL formed in March 1862 following the recent Confederate disaster at Fort Donelson, Tennessee. There, Brigadier General John Buchanan Floyd, a former United States Secretary of War, lost nearly all his command captured by Union forces in a blundering tactical operation. Typical of political appointees with no military experience, Floyd was popular and influential before the war, but a rather inept commander. He was also infamous for arranging the covert distribution of some 200,000 Federal muskets from Northern arsenals along with other war supplies, to Southern arsenals in 1859.[86]

Nonetheless, Union troops under Ulysses S. Grant routed Floyd at Fort Donelson, with only his Virginians escaping. Afterward, public outcry from the other states whose sons were captured there accused

Floyd of abandoning all but his Virginians, causing President Jefferson Davis to remove him from command. General John Floyd's censure was brief, however. His strong political ties in western Virginia created a backlash preventing Confederate President Jefferson Davis from dismissing him from the army altogether. His friends in the Virginia legislature were outraged following Floyd's removal, and began a flurry of petitions and political maneuvers seeking to restore him as a commander.[87]

Despite numerous historians denying that Devil Anse was ever in the 36th Virginia Infantry, and lack of evidence thereof in military records, Coleman Hatfield stated "The likelihood is that he fought with the Logan Wildcats [Company D] through the Fort Donelson campaign, and then returned home in time for the conception of his first child, Johnson "Johnse" Hatfield (January 6, 1862), who was named for William Johnson McCoy, one of Louvicey Chafin Hatfield's brothers-in-law. Anse probably remained with the Wildcats until February 1862 and then joined the Virginia State Line in order to protect his own."[88]

However, Johnson "Johnse" Hatfield was born on January 6, 1862. The 36th Virginia Infantry was at Bowling Green, Kentucky, on January 8, 1862 and moved to Russellville, Tennessee, on January 20, 1862, with the rest of General John Floyd's command. On February 2, 1862, Floyd's troops were sent to Cumberland City, Tennessee; on February 13, the 36th Virginia Infantry was ordered to Fort Donelson under Brigadier General John McCausland. When the fort fell, McCausland's troops moved to Chattanooga on February 25, where they remained until early April before being furloughed home until May 1.[89]

Soon afterward, the VSL formed on May 15, 1862, with Brigadier General John B. Floyd once again placed in command. This organization of state troops was intended to include all classes of white males not liable for service under the Confederate Conscription Act of April 6, 1862. While obviously a political vehicle for Floyd, its stated purpose was to protect the southwestern territories near the Kentucky and North Carolina borders of Virginia, where the citizens where quite divided as to North-South sympathies. The VSL was authorized to recruit two brigades of five regiments each.

Recruiting began June 4, 1862, and by August 5, 1862, Floyd had two regiments partially formed. During that summer the Pike County Kentucky area witnessed "bitter fighting" and in early August, a Confederate force, thought by many to have been Colonel Vincent Witcher and his 34th Battalion Virginia Cavalry, was involved in a skirmish along Peter Creek in Pike County with Union home guards.[90]

There were several Unionists in that area; when the Union army had established at least temporary control during that summer, many Union supporters joined a local home guard unit led by a prominent local official, William Francis, Jr., (also appears as "French" in some accounts) the same person who allegedly ordered Asa Harmon McCoy to fight Devil Anse in 1861, prompting him to enlist. (discussed in Chapter One). Francis owned 1,300 acres of land along the Tug River and operated a general store. Francis had recruited a company of approximately fifty-seven men, including three of Devil Anse's cousins: James, Joseph and Thompson Hatfield. This band was well known and feared among Southern citizens.[91]

Brigadier General John B. Floyd.
Library of Congress.

Francis was the captain, and his company was involved in numerous raids and skirmishes with Southern sympathizers and Union troops. Francis often worked alongside another Union home guard organization led by Captain Uriah Runyon, also of Peter Creek. One of the men in this company, Asa Harmon McCoy, would later become well known following his murder in 1865, which many believe was one of the causal factors in the famous Hatfield-McCoy feud. Each of the two companies formally aligned with the 167th Regiment Virginia Militia in September 1862, one of the few Union militia regiments in that region of western Virginia; however, they lacked adequate arms, and requested new ones from the state.[92]

Although possibly apocryphal, the Peter Creek home guard companies were said to have feared and respected Devil Anse, and considered him a "determined, deadly foe" due to his aggressive, tenacious spirit and reputation as a crack marksman.[93]

Meanwhile, Brigadier General John Floyd was recruiting in earnest for his new command, the VSL. He offered potential recruits one-year enlistments as an incentive, as opposed to regular Confederate service which was then three years, or the duration of the war. There was also a promise that they would serve primarily in the mountainous regions near their homes, not to mention the extra incentive that "...property taken from the enemy will be equally distributed among those capturing it."[94]

Devil Anse enlisted in the 2nd Regiment, VSL, as a private in July 1862. He was soon commissioned as a 1st Lieutenant of Cavalry in Company G, 2nd Regiment, VSL, on September 20, 1862. The 2nd Regiment included ten companies of both infantry and cavalry, although Hatfield was not in the cavalry element.[95]

Hatfield served under Captain James R. Cook from Wyoming County, where most of the men in the company were from. Many of those seventy-one troops had also served in the 187th Regiment Virginia Militia, and had earlier fought at the battle of Barboursville in July 1861. Shortly after enlisting in July, the newly formed companies of the VSL rendezvoused at Camp Moore located in Abb's Valley, south of Flat Top Mountain in Tazewell County, Virginia.[96]

Colonel Elisha Peters collected a task force of one hundred men from the 2nd VSL Regiment on August 19, 1862, and ordered them to prepare to march with three days rations and forty rounds of ammunition. The detachment moved out to the Tug Fork area August 20 and bivouacked near Elkhorn Creek that night. The next day, Colonel Peters force-marched the detachment toward the pinnacle of the Guyandotte River.[97]

There they found an unsuspecting Union detachment from the 5th Kentucky Infantry, who were eating breakfast in their camp. The Confederates attacked, catching the Federals by surprise, and captured three prisoners, two horses, and twenty-one rifles along with various supplies and food stores. Then, Colonel Peters returned his detachment to their camp on August 22, 1862.[98]

The 2nd VSL next moved to Salt Lick in Dickinson County, Virginia, where they encamped and began holding regular drills to improve discipline. A few days later, they moved to Jeffersonville, where the regiment encamped for about ten days before marching through Wyoming County. Their trek ended at Logan on October 1, 1862, where they drilled, and spent "considerable time fishing."[99]

The bulk of other VSL troops also arrived at Logan soon thereafter. The Logan-Pikeville region was then experiencing a high frequency of "bushwhacking" by both Union and Confederate guerrillas, as well as attacks by home guards in the area. Bushwhackers were often indistinguishable from home guards or guerrilla units; these small, but deadly, forces preyed upon both regular troops and civilians, and many of the men in such units were said to have conducted personal vendettas against the families of men serving on the side opposite their own.

These groups operated independently without financial or logistical support from the government and were not bound by accepted laws of warfare. Hence, on the one hand, they could do as they pleased to their enemies, but if captured, military commanders who saw them as a menace could, in theory, simply execute them as criminals rather than prisoners of war. Many were captured on both sides and imprisoned, however, and such executions, while not uncommon, were rarely documented beyond soldier accounts found in their diaries or letters.

Four companies composed mainly of Irishmen (including Hatfield's Company G) from the 2nd Regiment VSL were sent to Warfield, Kentucky, on October 12, 1862. There they engaged in a substantial fight with three hundred Union home guards. When the Confederates attacked, the Union men quickly "took to the hills" and were pursued through the town. One Confederate officer was shocked to find several Unionist women there who "…fired guns at us from the windows."[100]

The Confederates chased the retreating Federals roughly three miles outside city limits, to a point with several rocky hillsides where they took cover. Floyd's men patiently waited and brought up their artillery that night. The next morning, Floyd found large groups of Federal soldiers trying to escape from the rocky crevices on the hillside above him and ordered the artillery to open fire. An eyewitness described Floyd's troops at that time as "well clad, well-armed, with plenty of provisions, and in good spirits."[101]

When the cannons fired, they used ordnance known as "grape shot," which were solid lead or steel balls weighing anywhere from one to six pounds each, tightly packed into a canvas bag and primed with gunpowder. As the round discharged, it created a vicious close-range effect like a shotgun, creating a potentially deadly weapon against infantry. However, the effects here were minimal, described as having only "…trimmed up the trees considerably," as the Federals scampered deeper into the hills. Afterward, Floyd's expedition returned to Logan on or about October 19, 1862.[102]

Once again encamped at Logan, soldiers in the VSL found there was little "…real military duty to be done…some of the men spent considerable time fishing while in Logan County." In late October 1862, another expedition was sent to New Garden, in Russell County, Virginia. They stayed only a few days, although the weather turned into a heavy snow, which Floyd made the men march through upon their return to Logan.[103]

In mid-November 1862, General John Floyd informed Virginia Governor John Letcher the VSL would soon begin to experience food shortages at Logan; it was also the first time Floyd had managed to amass his entire command at one location. He then had four regiments now divided into two brigades, with the 1st and 2nd VSL comprising the 1st Brigade and continued to order patrols and expeditions into the eastern Kentucky area.

On November 14, 1862, Floyd's 1st Brigade marched from Chapmanville along the Guyandotte River toward Cabell County "over a rough and difficult road." The next day they encountered a Federal detachment near Guyandotte, which was quickly "routed and dispensed."[104]

As the expedition neared the Ohio River, they found numerous Union home guard units and easily routed them. Passing through Wayne County on November 16, 1862, Floyd attacked the Union garrison there comprised of several companies from the 5th West Virginia Infantry, and quickly dispersed them after a short skirmish. Afterward, Floyd had several local citizens with known Union sympathies arrested.[105]

Near the end of November, the 39th Kentucky Mounted Infantry Regiment under Colonel John Dils took post along the Big Sandy River. Dils hoped to secure several large coal boats for use by the Union army. His regiment was comprised mainly of men from eastern Kentucky and southwestern Virginia. This outfit drew the unparalleled ire of many soldiers in VSL, as many were friends and acquaintances, and in some instances, family before the war. General Floyd sent Colonel John M. Clarkson of the 3rd VSL with a force comprised of 800 troops from the 1st, 2nd and 3rd VSL, from Ceredo in Wayne County, Virginia, into Kentucky looking for the Federals.[106]

Clarkson arrived in the area known as Wireman's Shoals in Floyd County, Kentucky, on the evening of December 3, 1862. The shoals were near where the 39th Kentucky was diligently working on the coal boats. In a bold move, Clarkson ordered a general charge against the surprised Federals. The sudden massed attack caused many to run for cover inside of the boats, as the Confederates made a furious charge.

The Union troops left on land were barely able to "get off one good volley" at Floyd's men before being surrounded, as he had earlier sent a large detachment behind the Federals that caught them completely unaware. The disorganized Unionists offered some slight resistance afterward, but eventually broke and retreated.[107]

The Confederates had fourteen to fifteen casualties in the raid, while the Federals lost twenty men killed or wounded. Floyd also recaptured nearly a quarter million dollars in Confederate monies that was taken earlier in the war, along with much needed supplies including five hundred "splendid" overcoats, five hundred Austrian Rifles, five hundred pairs of pants, five hundred pairs of flannel underwear, five hundred hats, eight hundred pairs of shoes, and three thousand pairs of socks.[108]

Afterward, the 1st Brigade quickly moved to the heights along Bull Mountain, near Piketon, Kentucky, and waited on the retreating Federals. Two days later they had another brief skirmish with Colonel Dil's men, lasting about one hour before the demoralized Union troops again retreated.[109]

During this expedition, Devil Anse was said to have been present with Colonel John M. Clarkson's force. During the return march to Logan, the command brought along twenty-five prisoners, one of whom was Asa Harmon McCoy, who was captured while recovering from a gunshot wound, when VSL men surrounded his home on December 5, 1862.[110]

Family tradition claims that Devil Anse learned from one of the Union prisoners that a slave named Mose from the Jacob Cline family had placed a bounty of twenty-five dollars on him. It is unlikely Mose could have done so, however, because Virginia law did not allow slaves to have money. Jacob Cline's youngest son, Perry, later proved to be Hatfield's arch enemy during the feud years, however.[111]

After the Civil War, Cline family tradition posited that Hatfield was party to a later raid on the Cline home that nearly cost the lives of Mose and Jacob Cline, and allegedly captured Randall McCoy in the process, although he was a prisoner at Camp Chase, Ohio from July 1863 until the end of the war. Another source claims Devil Anse had shot Mose and killed him in a later raid during the winter 1862-1863, although it remains undocumented beyond oral tradition.[112]

However, Peter Cline and Mose were both later identified as members of several partisan raids attacking Confederate troops in the area and were considered lawful combatants. Ultimately, Hatfield's presence at Asa Harmon McCoy's capture on December 5, 1862 is circumstantial at best, along with other subsequent raids on the Cline family.[113]

After the expedition, Floyd's command returned to the mouth of Pond Creek, just south of Williamson, Virginia (later West Virginia) where they planned to re-enter winter quarters on December 7, 1862. However, the idleness of winter encampment had little time to grip the soldiers, as Floyd soon again ordered the entire force out on a scouting mission into Cabell County near Guyandotte spanning the next two weeks.[114]

Enroute, the 2nd Regiment VSL had another small skirmish with some Ohio troops near Catlettsburg, Kentucky, on December 17. There were no casualties in that affair. During this march, Floyd passed through Barboursville, Wayne Court House, and then crossed over the river into Louisa, Kentucky.

Next, they moved along the western fork of the Sandy River to Rock Castle, and then crossed over the mountains to Warfield and returned to Logan, covering about one hundred forty miles on the dangerous winter expedition. One participant noted, "...scarcely a day passed that skulking bushwhackers did not attack some portion of our column." Afterward the VSL returned to Russell County, Virginia, where it remained until January 1863.[115]

The majority of VSL troops relocated to Saltville, Virginia in January 1863. This was ostensibly to help protect the extensive salt works located there, which the Confederate government desperately needed for manufacturing gunpowder. Few of the soldiers involved then likely realized, however, that the salt works were not government owned. Rather, the owner was none other than their shrewd commander, Brigadier General John B. Floyd, who was bent on protecting his own personal interests as much as aiding the Southern cause.[116]

The next few weeks were generally quiet for the VSL; one of General John Floyd's staff officers described the winter lull as "mud, rain and idleness." This was not the case for enlisted VSL men, however, as a few days after arriving at Saltville, the 1st Brigade VSL troops were ordered to manual labor, constructing a large network of earthen breastworks lining the hillside around the town. Despite the winter camp doldrums, Floyd often sent small patrols into Kentucky to seize horses and other livestock from Unionists and attempt to destroy a few small groups of Union guerrillas or irregulars still present in the Tug Valley.[117]

While there were certainly no large battles in the area at the time, there was often violence involved on patrols and raids. One of Floyd's lieutenants, a young staff officer named Micajah Woods, who was raised in a wealthy eastern Virginia family, was stunned by the bitter and personal nature of the violence he witnessed along the eastern Kentucky and western Virginia border. Woods recalled,

> No person reared in the full light of our Eastern Virginia civilization can form a remote conception of the condition of the counties through which we passed and their inhabitants. To subdue the people, the houses of the greater portion of the Southern men have been committed to flames, and their families thrown out into the dreary world, homeless, destitute and penniless. Neighbor against neighbor - the roads are waylaid, and in many communities the men have not slept in their own houses for months past, but have pursued a course of life termed 'laying out' in the gorges of the mountains waiting for opportunities to slay some solitary or personal opponent.[118]

Another detachment from Hatfield's brigade was sent to Glade Springs, Virginia on January 4, 1863, where scouts had found a force of Federal cavalry lurking near Pound Gap. No contact was had, however, and they returned to camp. During the winter authorities at Richmond came to view the VSL as an embarrassment to both the Virginia and Confederate governments. Authorities received many complaints about brawls between enlisted men and officers, and that VSL troops were stealing livestock and horses, as well as slaves, and looting farmhouses.[119]

It appears this largely had to do with the fact that VSL officers failed to maintain rigid military discipline due to the constituency of rugged and unruly mountaineers who refused to adapt their mindset to military structure. It probably didn't help that most of them were also from the same communities; however, most were "more concerned with themselves than their men" according to one source.[120]

However, poor discipline also led to poor morale, which in turn caused desertions. This problem piqued when the soldiers learned that command of the VSL troops was being transferred from the state to the Confederate government. By March 3, 1863, Colonel Alfred Beckley's regiment appeared to have melted away overnight from men eloping.[121]

1st Lieutenant Micajah Woods observed, "I am not at all astonished at the course of these men. They are principally from the border – a region occupied or at the mercy of the enemy – their wifes and families in the majority of cases are helpless and destitute of the absolute necessities of life, and worse than this are subject [to] the insults and depredations of the marauding parties of each side that infest their whole country."[122]

With his reputation already tarnished in the eyes of many government authorities from the 1862 disaster at Fort Donelson, when VSL desertions escalated, along with scandals involving General Floyd misappropriating government funds, the previously indulgent state authorities could take no more. When Floyd failed to account for several thousand dollars which he received under the pretense of procuring much needed supplies and arms for his men, it was the straw that broke the camel's back.

Political pressure against General Floyd became so great that the state government decided to disband the VSL in February 1863. Rumors flew for several weeks as to whether the VSL troops would be transferred into the regular Confederate army or be allowed to return home.[123]

Desertions also continued as morale sank even further. Despite the accusations flurrying around him, Floyd remained popular with most of his troops. Most desertions in this period, however, appear to have also been fueled by the realization that most of the men would end up serving in regular Confederate units even farther away from their homes in the eastern theatre.[124]

Another factor was that a deep resentment emerged toward officers who refused to allow furloughs for soldiers to visit their families amidst daily reports of harassment by Union troops in the Tug River Valley, and rumors of a large Union force gathering in Tennessee with plans to enter Kentucky and southwestern Virginia.

Their aggravation is not surprising, as officers often awarded themselves furloughs lasting over a month, in anticipation of the VSL's demise. This allowed them plenty of time to acquire positions in other commands or to negotiate political appointments while the fate of their men hung in limbo. The VSL were officially disbanded April 1, 1863, and the men were then given indefinite furloughs until the government decided what to do with them.[125]

Devil Anse Hatfield.
Public Domain.

3

1863: 45th Battalion Virginia Infantry

One writer asserted that Devil Anse joined Company D, 1st Regiment of the 45th Battalion Virginia Infantry as a private in 1861, although the regiment was not formed until 1863. There is no evidence that Hatfield was ever a member of Company D; rather, service records show he enlisted as a private in Company B, 45th Battalion Virginia Infantry, a few days after the VSL disbanded in April 1863.[126]

This regiment contained the bulk of men formerly serving in the 1st Brigade VSL with Hatfield; many were also former members of the 36th Virginia Infantry. Enlisting in this regiment was evidence of Devil Anse's willingness to fight, particularly considering the scandals and poor morale in the late VSL. He was also likely influenced by learning that his friend and former neighbor, Captain John Buchanan, who formerly commanded Company I, VSL, was to command Company B. Another potential reason was that the highly respected former VSL staff officer and Lieutenant Colonel of the 36th Virginia Infantry, Henry M. Beckley, was to be Colonel of the new regiment.

Beckley was also a former member of Company D, 36th Virginia

Infantry, a.k.a. the "Logan Wildcats," which may account for why several authors have incorrectly assumed Devil Anse was also in that company. For example, one researcher erroneously claimed Hatfield served in Company A, 45th Battalion Virginia Infantry, and adding to the confusion also stated that company was known as the Logan Wildcats. Another historian wrote that Hatfield had enlisted in Company D, 45th Battalion Virginia Infantry in 1861, which could not possibly be true, as the regiment did not exist until 1863.[127]

The men in Company B hailed mainly from Logan and Wyoming Counties, where roughly three percent of the population were slaveholders, according to the 1860 U.S. Census. Enlistments were completed for ninety-seven former VSL men in Company B on May 7, 1863 in Logan and Smythe Counties, Virginia.[128]

45th Battalion Virginia Infantry flag. Courtesy American Civil War Museum (formerly Museum of the Confederacy, Richmond, Virginia). This flag was carried until May 9, 1864, when Colonel Isaac Duval of the 9th West Virginia Infantry captured it during the battle of Cloyd's Mountain, near Dublin, Virginia. Devil Anse Hatfield was not present during that battle.

Hatfield's leadership was again recognized soon after his enlistment, despite former alliances with General John Floyd. He was elected 1st Lieutenant, and his younger brother, Ellison Hatfield, was elected 2nd Lieutenant, his immediate subordinate. Oral tradition holds that Devil Anse was later promoted to captain of this company, but muster rolls and service records do not bear this out. Nearly all the men in Company B were former members of Company I, 1st Regiment VSL, where Ellison had served under Captain John Buchanan.[129]

Colonel Beckley's new recruits were sent to Saltville where he formed his command throughout the month of June. While there, the 45th Battalion was assigned to the 2nd Brigade, Army of Western Virginia, under Brigadier General John S. Williams along with the 63rd Virginia Infantry, 21st Virginia Cavalry, and Lowry's Battery of Artillery. This brigade was under overall command of Major General Samuel Jones.[130]

Battle at Pond Creek

Their first actions as an organized unit were engaging in several patrols and scouting expeditions in the Logan, Wyoming and Pike County areas and arresting many Union citizens. It did not take long to encounter Federal troops, however, and their first combat occurred on July 6, 1863. As part of a larger plan to thrust Union troops into the heart of Confederate states led by Major General Ambrose E. Burnside, Brigadier General Julius White moved a brigade of approximately 1,100 troops into Pike County on July 6, 1863. Bringing detachments from the 39th Kentucky Infantry and two companies of the 69th Illinois Infantry, he scouted to the Tug River intending to disperse Captain John Buchanan's company, of which Devil Anse was 1st Lieutenant.[131]

White divided his force in half and sent a detachment toward Gladesville, in Wise County, Virginia, bent on diverting the enemy attention away from a movement of Union troops, demonstrating in the direction of Saltville, Virginia, on July 1, 1863. As the 39th Kentucky under Colonel John Dils and two companies of the 69th Illinois Infantry approached the Virginia border on July 3, 1863, they moved from Pikeville to Louisa Fork, in Louisa County, Kentucky, on the Sandy River and encountered Confederates enroute, which included the 45th Battalion Virginia Infantry.[132]

General White later reported, "I detached…the remaining force, to attempt to capture a body of the enemy on the Tug Fork, some 25 miles distant…" The force White found was Captain John Buchanan's Company B, 45th Battalion Virginia Infantry, with about one hundred men. The Federals bivouacked along Pond Creek (probably on the Pike County, Kentucky side) on the night of July 5, 1863.

Overnight, Buchanan's company moved forward to reconnoiter Pond Creek, where scouts earlier located Federal troops. Upon approaching the Union detachment, they quickly engaged in a sharp fight lasting several hours. White later reported that his men counterattacked the Confederates by "…boldly charging up the mountainside with the greatest gallantry."[133]

White also noted his troops "routed and dispersed the enemy under Buchanan, killing 5 and capturing 20. The enemy took to the cliffs and mountain sides, but the brave Illinoisans and Kentuckians vied with each other in climbing the steps under a galling fire and driving the enemy from their mountain fastness."[134]

As usual, Union and Confederate accounts of the engagement contradicted each other. The *Lynchburg Virginian* newspaper printed an account of the battle written by an unidentified member of Hatfield's company on July 18, 1863, entitled "A Fight in Western Virginia" as follows:

> A correspondent writing from Logan County gives the particulars of a fight which occurred there on the 9th inst. He says: We had a severe brush with the enemy today. The notorious Col. Dils sent one hundred men to destroy the crops etc., on Mate Creek, which empties into the Tug River about 20 miles above Warfield on the Va. side. The vandals succeeded in capturing several horses on the creek and destroying the residences of Capt. Buchanan and a few others. Capt. Buchanan hastily rallied a portion of this company, together with Capt.

Walker's, and attacked the enemy whilst still in his work of destruction.

He killed six of the enemy upon the field, wounded some 25 and utterly routed the remainder. Our loss two killed and a few wounded. All praise to the noble Buchanan and his brave men! Logan County, be it remembered together with Boone, Wyoming, Cabell, Putnam, McDowell and Buchanan are claimed to belong to the state of "West Virginia."

Yet, these counties have a brigade of cavalry under Gen. [Albert G.] Jenkins and a full regiment of infantry under Gen. [John] McCausland. Besides these, the gallant Col. [Henry] Beckley is rapidly organizing a new regiment of infantry, principally in Logan, Boone and Wyoming.

These gallant mountain men leave their plows and families to the care of Heaven, and rush to arms in defense of the Old Commonwealth. Such examples of patriotism and self-sacrifice are few and far between. God speed the cause!" One of the Union soldiers killed in the fight at Pond Creek was Captain Uriah Runyon, who led a company of home guards from Peter Creek in Pike County, a former neighbor of many of the Confederates engaged there.[135]

Randall McCoy Captured by Union Troops

The Official Records of the action at Pond Creek on July 7, 1863, state the Federal troops, comprised of a detachment of the 65th Illinois Infantry and 39th Kentucky Infantry, accomplished their mission to disperse "...the enemy, under Buchanan..." Records from Camp Chase, Ohio indicate Randolph (Randall) McCoy, who was later Devil Anse's antagonist during the feud era, was captured in eastern Kentucky on July 8, 1863, and arrived there on August 22, 1863.[136]

McCoy later transferred to Camp Douglas, Illinois, where he remained until taking the Oath of Allegiance on June 16, 1865. Rolls from Camp Douglas also note he was affiliated with "Co. C, Beckley's Regt" which is the 45th Battalion Virginia Infantry. Since Buchanan's Company was in fact present at Pond Creek, and Randall McCoy was captured in the area one day later, some authors concluded that he was in the 45th Battalion Virginia Infantry, although feud writers often disagree on this issue. One author indicated that Randall McCoy had no military service, although cited a blank page in the source; other feud accounts assert that McCoy was a Union supporter, but while that has no factual basis, several Unionists were among Randall McCoy's strongest supporters during the feud.[137]

[Left] Prisoner of War record and [Right] Oath of Allegiance for Randolph (Randall) McCoy. National Archives, Washington, D.C.

A Case of Mistaken Identity?

Two researchers also recently cautioned that it is uncertain whether the Randolph McCoy found in military records is the famous feudist, because he had a cousin by the same name. Neither source offers any information as to who the cousin was, however. Feudist Randolph McCoy, Sr., was born on October 30, 1825. He married his first cousin, Sarah "Sally" McCoy (b. 1829), the daughter of Samuel McCoy and Elizabeth Davis, on December 9, 1849. The non-feudist cousin with the same name was aged thirty-two years in 1860, five years younger than the feud patriarch. He married Elizabeth Sansum (Sessum) on April 16, 1846 in Pike County, Kentucky. They resided in Logan County, [West Virginia] and feudist Randall McCoy, Sr., lived in Pike County, Kentucky, in 1860.[138]

As noted, military records from the 45th Battalion Virginia Infantry, Virginia State Line Cavalry and Infantry Regiments and 10th Kentucky Cavalry do not show Randall McCoy on their rolls. Another potentially discerning factor is that McCoy family tradition says the non-feudist cousin was known as "Black Rannel" McCoy. The same family tradition also claims it was Black Rannel, not the feudist, who participated in the raid against Pikeville Unionist Peter Cline. The Cline family tradition also contends it was Black Rannel. (Discussed in Chapter Two) During the fight, Black Rannel was supposedly clubbed with a rifle by one of their family slaves named Mose. Family tradition is tentative at best, but given these factors, it is doubtful that Black Rannel was the same Randall McCoy who was captured on July 8, 1863 noted in Confederate service records. Another factor is a civil court case Randall McCoy, Sr., filed against Devil Anse in Lawrence County in 1892. Hatfield testified in this litigation that he served with Randall McCoy in the 45th Battalion Virginia Infantry and made no mention of Black Rannel. Overall, while we cannot be certain, the Randall McCoy captured in eastern Kentucky on July 8, 1863, in eastern Kentucky was most likely the later feudist.[139]

More Questions about McCoy's Service

Prison records also reflect Randall McCoy had three other unit affiliations, including "Co. A, May's Virginia Cavalry," which was the 10th Kentucky Cavalry (Confederate) commanded by Colonel Andrew Jackson May, and also "1 Cav State Line" [1st Regiment Cavalry, Virginia State Line] and "1 Inf Va State Line," [1st Regiment Infantry, Virginia State Line]. However, none of those organization's muster rolls or related service records contain McCoy's name.[140]

Like the 45th Battalion, Virginia State Line records, records from the 10th Kentucky Cavalry; 10th Kentucky Mounted Rifles; and the 13th Kentucky Cavalry, do not contain Randall McCoy's name. Comprised mainly of men from the Tug Fork Valley in eastern Kentucky, the 10th Kentucky Cavalry (Confederate) was initially commanded by Colonel Andrew Jackson May. Later, the regimental commanders were Colonel Edwin Trimble and George R. Diamond, successively. Hence, it is often referred to as Mays, Trimble's or Diamond's Regiment depending on the time period. Note that May's regiment is sometimes confused with Colonel Benjamin E. Caudill's 13th Kentucky Cavalry, which was also known as the 10th Kentucky Mounted Rifles, or in some records, appears as the 10th Kentucky Mounted Infantry.[141]

Ironically, Coleman Hatfield, who in his popular book, *Tale of the Devil*, erroneously wrote that Devil Anse served in the Logan Wildcats, makes no mention of Randall McCoy serving with Devil Anse in the 45th Battalion Virginia Infantry. Still another common but inaccurate account found in the feud literature is that Randall McCoy served in Devil Anse Hatfield's partisan guerrilla company during 1864-1865. One writer even claimed that Randall McCoy was partly responsible for the death of his brother, Asa Harmon McCoy in January 1865, although Randall was incarcerated at Camp Douglas, Illinois, until June 16, 1865.[142]

Devil Anse's former daughter-in-law, Sadie Click, (ex-spouse of Tennis Hatfield), also indicated during a May 15, 1988 interview with the *Floyd County Times* that Randall McCoy was once a member of

Randall McCoy, Sr.
Public Domain.

Hatfield's late war partisan company "for a short time," but left because "he soon grew tired of Anse's stern discipline." Interestingly, Mrs. Click also told the reporter that she never feared Devil Anse or any of the other feudists, because she could "outshoot any of the men and was just as mean as they were." However, as Randall was in a Union prison after July 8, 1863, the story is apocryphal.[143]

On the other hand, there are other McCoys identified as members of the 45th Battalion Virginia Infantry muster rolls, including five who served with Devil Anse in Captain John Buchanan's Company B. Only two of the McCoy feudists sided with the Hatfields during the feud, however. (Appendix Table 2) Some were also former neighbors living near both Hatfield and Buchanan according to the 1860 U.S. Census. Recall that John Buchanan also led one of the companies of the 129th Regiment Virginia Militia in 1861, although his brother Thomas Buchanan, a Union supporter, also led a company in that regiment during the antebellum era. John Buchanan also later commanded a company in both the Virginia State Line, and later 45th Battalion Infantry, comprised of many of the same men including Devil Anse and some of the McCoy family.[144]

Hatfield and McCoy family tradition alike holds that Devil Anse was always friends with Randall McCoy, even during the feud he was said to have liked him; rather it was toward McCoy's sons whom Hatfield directed his ire. The notion of the two patriarchs as friends and comrades in the Confederate army was further boosted by an article appearing in the *Logan Banner* newspaper on December 2, 1938. That organ contained an anecdotal report that the two had worked together on a raid on the home of Captain William "Yankee Bill" Francis, the Union home guard commander from Peter Creek, in Pike County, whom Randall McCoy's brother Asa Harmon served with. The incident is thought to have occurred sometime during mid to late 1863.[145]

The *Logan Banner* account also claims that Captain John Buchanan had ordered Hatfield to organize a detail of men, said to include Randall McCoy, and go after Yankee Bill Francis, taking him "dead or alive." During the raid on Francis's home, one of the attackers shot and killed him. Several writers have suggested it was Devil Anse who pulled the trigger, although that is conjectural. A problem with this version is that in spite of the many researchers who claim it as evidence that Devil Anse and Randall McCoy served together in the same Confederate unit, two historians more credibly argue the incident occurred in late 1864 or early 1865, and as noted, Randall McCoy was in a Union prison from July 7, 1863, until the end of the war.[146]

Devil Anse's Home Burned by Union Troops

A series of many other similar raids also occurred in the Tug Valley region during 1863, showing further how deeply rooted the resentment between Union and Confederates were in the region. Devil Anse was said to have been involved in raids on no less than nineteen Unionist homes in the Peter Creek area during this era of service, although that is based on oral and family tradition. Yet, nearly all of those nineteen families had men serving in the 167th Regiment Virginia Militia or Union home guard units including Captain William "Yankee Bill" Francis, his son James M. Francis, his son-in-law John Charles, and brother-in-law William Trigg Cline, as well as Asa Harmon McCoy.[147]

Illustrating the depth of sectionalist conflict that existed in western Virginia and eastern Kentucky, there were numerous post-war lawsuits filed in Pike County, Kentucky, naming several men from Union home guard units as responsible for plundering Southern families in Pike and Logan Counties. The Union home guards operating along the Kentucky border were described by a Confederate veteran as creating "a terror" among the Southern residents.[148]

If factual, one reported raid likely had more to do with Devil Anse's ire toward Union soldiers as any, because it was against his own family. The writer recalled, "...about 1863, a party of men as such always infests border territory went to his house and in a most brutal manner burned his family out. Nor was this near all the indignities to which they were subjected. On hearing this, Hatfield secured leave of absence from the army, and promptly settled with the villains."[149]

Muster rolls from the 45th Battalion Virginia Infantry fail to show Devil Anse took leave in July 1863, but he was not the only man whose family suffered from Federal raids that summer. Also, the home of his friend and commanding officer, Captain John Buchanan, was burned and his family harassed just days before, again reinforcing the animosity present in the Tug River Valley region during the Civil War.[150]

Because both Hatfield and Captain John Buchanan were not only neighbors, but also well-known members of the Mate's Creek community as well as Confederate officers, there was doubtlessly a strong incentive on the part of Union troops to attack both homes on the same series of raids. It seems very unlikely that only Buchanan's home would have been attacked under those circumstances.[151]

The 39th Kentucky Mounted Infantry and 65th Illinois Mounted Infantry were then under command of Colonel John Dils, a native of Pike County, Kentucky. Dils gained a fearsome reputation in the area for his attacks on the families of Confederate soldiers, and he was doubtless well acquainted with both Buchanan and Devil Anse.[152]

Colonel John Dils, circa 1876.
Courtesy of Pikeville County Museum.

When Captain John Buchanan received word that Union troops were raiding farms near his own, he reportedly took a party of men from Company B and caught Dils' raiders red-handed in the act of destroying his home. One does not have to indulge much of a leap in logic to imagine the rage and fear he must have experienced upon witnessing that event. They were said to have ensured that the aftermath did not go well for the Union home guards, who managed to take a few horses before Buchanan and his men arrived and "killed six of the enemy upon the field, wounded some twenty-five, and utterly routed the remainder. Our loss, two killed and a few wounded." The reader should note, however, that often accounts of such incidents are exaggerated.[153]

In this instance, service records do not mention any deaths occurring in the 45th Battalion during the expedition despite the *Lynchburg Virginian* account suggesting there were two men killed and five wounded. Also, in contrast to Colonel Dils' official report, the 45th Battalion rolls fail to show that there were twenty men captured; rather, only six of Buchanan's men were captured there.[154]

In spite of discrepant accounts of the raid, it is likely Devil Anse and his comrades knew they were fighting against many of the men in the 39th Kentucky Mounted Infantry who formerly served with them in the Virginia State Line, including some of the McCoy family. It is not unreasonable to think such dynamics would only reinforce the already agitated sectionalist tensions and burn into a deep resentment that continued during the reconstruction era.

It is further noted that the 45th Battalion then contained at least thirty men who resided in the Pikeville, Kentucky area, and they were undoubtedly familiar with Colonel John Dils also, who was a popular merchant prior to the war. That scenario further embodies the very personal and embittered nature of the Civil War in the Tug River Valley region. While those small raids meant little, if anything, to the larger theaters of war, the families and soldiers involved would not soon forget them.[155]

The Gettysburg Myth

On a larger scale, the summer of 1863 was a pivotal point in the Civil War; on July 1-3 at Gettysburg, Pennsylvania, the Union army defeated Confederates under Robert E. Lee, causing the army to retreat into Virginia. Also, on July 4, the Confederate stronghold at Vicksburg, Mississippi fell to General Ulysses S. Grant after nearly two months of siege warfare. This era also produced one of the most popular, but mythical, tales in the feud literature. This version supposes that Devil Anse's subordinate officer and younger brother, 2nd Lieutenant Ellison Hatfield, who served with him in Company B, 45th Battalion Virginia Infantry, was at the battle of Gettysburg. This is contradicted by military records, however.[156]

One such story appears in Truda McCoy's book, *The McCoys: Their Story as told by Eyewitnesses and Descendants*. Citing historian Leonard Roberts, that author claimed Ellison "fought for the Confederacy from the heroic stand at Gettysburg to surrender with Robert E. Lee at Appomattox." The same account is also cited by Dr. Altina Waller in her 1988 seminal study, *Feud: Hatfields, McCoys and Social Change in Appalachia, 1860-1900*.[157]

In addition, one author wrote that Ellison Hatfield had even served at Gettysburg, "all the time of the struggle July 14, 1863", but the Gettysburg campaign began in June 1863, and the battle occurred on July 1-3, 1863. Despite the glorious legend, military records and other reliable sources place Ellison Hatfield with the 45th Battalion in the Logan and Pikeville area during June 1863 and July 1-7, 1863. Obviously, neither Devil Anse nor Ellison Hatfield could have been at Gettysburg.[158]

While Devil Anse named one of his sons after the famous general who commanded troops at Gettysburg and other major battles, Robert E. Lee, there is no evidence either he or Ellison were at Gettysburg or ever served on a campaign under his direct command. Note that Hatfield also named another son after William Johnson McCoy, who served with him in the 45th Battalion. The latter was his brother-in-law, and a member of Company E.[159]

As the summer of 1863 progressed, the 45th Battalion Virginia Infantry next returned to Saltville in anticipation of a Federal attack that

Ellison Hatfield in uniform.
West Virginia State Archives.

never happened. The regiment marched to Camp Georgia at Jeffersonville in Tazewell County, Virginia on July 17, 1863, where they learned that a Union force of about 1,300 Union troops were stationed at nearby Abb's Valley. As part of a larger operation aimed at cutting off the vital Virginia & Tennessee railroad in southwestern Virginia, the Federals were also busy raiding and burning farms and a few houses near Wytheville, taking many horses from Southern sympathizers as well. Hatfield's regiment deployed there in response and engaged Union troops at the base of Walker's Mountain on July 17, 1863.

The brief skirmish there resulted in eight Federals killed, twenty captured, along with some civilians including slaves. Three men of the 45th Battalion were killed. Afterward, the 45th Battalion returned to Camp Georgia, and remained there until August 28, 1863, when they returned to Saltville.[160]

While encamped there, provisions ran low once more, and Devil Anse signed receipts for new clothing items for his company, including drawers, shirts, uniform jackets, socks, and cooking utensils from the quartermaster department in Richmond. On August 31, 1863, Devil Anse again signed for receipt of two A Tents, tent flies, one camp kettle, two skillet lids, an axe, and an axe handle.[161]

On or about September 1, 1863, the 45th Battalion was encamped on the Kentucky-Virginia border. At that time, Major General Ambrose Burnside's Union army was moving northward from Knoxville, and had several skirmishes in eastern Tennessee; however, Hatfield's unit was not involved in any of those actions.[162]

During mid-September, thirteen men deserted from Company F. Colonel Alfred Beckley believed they went home, and planned to capture them as well as recruit new men once the 45th Battalion returned to the Logan area on or about October 1, 1863. Unit muster rolls show that one of Devil Anse's brothers, Private Elias Hatfield, enlisted in company B on May 7, 1863. He was reported as Absent Without Leave (AWOL) sometime during the period October 5 through 15, 1863 while at Logan. His service records indicate that he was "never paid" which potentially explains his departure; however, oddly, a later entry on the November – December 1864 company B roll states he was "home on sick leave since May 1, 1864."[163]

Service records for Devil Anse's other brother, 2nd Lieutenant Ellison Hatfield, give conflicting information as to when he deserted. A company B muster roll from April 1, 1864 shows him present; there are no further records until a December 31, 1864 company B muster roll which shows him Absent without Leave (AWOL) since December 19, 1864. That roll also notes he received pay on June 30, 1864, so it appears Ellison stayed on duty until December 19, 1864. After that, his commander requested that Division Headquarters drop him from rolls on January 30, 1865, (it must have become clear he was not going to return) which was done on March 3, 1865. Ellison Hatfield then took the Oath of Allegiance at Charleston on May 4, 1865.[164]

Devil Anse, Ellison and Smith Hatfield.
West Virginia State Archives.

Devil Anse Deserts

With one of his brothers gone, and hearing of troubles at home, it seems unlikely that Devil Anse stayed in camp much longer if at all. A December 1863 muster roll indicates only that he was missing since "____20, 1863." A muster roll of April 1, 1864 states he was identified as a deserter by February 1, 1864. With missing data on the rolls, it is not clear as to precisely when Devil Anse also deserted, but it appears he left during or before December 20, 1863.[165]

Recall also that in his 1889 interview with the *Wheeling Intelligencer*, Devil Anse offered a different explanation for his departure from the 45th Battalion, "I resigned in 1863, and then recruited a company which was kept in service in Wayne, Cabell, and other border counties of West Virginia and Kentucky." Devil Anse may well have tried to resign, although service records do not indicate evidence of such. Of course, when he claimed to have resigned, Hatfield probably did not consider that his service records, which clearly show he deserted, would later become a matter of public record.[166]

Hence, since we cannot be certain when Devil Anse or Ellison left, we similarly cannot be certain they were present for subsequent operations such as on October 18, 1863. On this date, Colonel Alfred Beckley learned that approximately three hundred Federal troops from the 2nd West Virginia Cavalry and 34th Ohio Mounted Infantry, under Brigadier General A.N. Duffie, were approaching the town from Charleston in search of his troops. On October 21 he marched the battalion towards Boone Court House to meet them. Federals arrived there between 12 noon and 3 p.m. that day.[167]

General Duffie reported, "Having arrived at that place, I found no enemy except a few stragglers, who were captured..." A few shots were fired rounding up the stragglers, but otherwise the trip was uneventful. Duffie further wrote, "I discovered that the information on which the movement was made was mainly without foundation, there having been at no time recently more than 15 or 20 rebels at Boone Court-House, or over 150 in the whole county."[168]

Duffie continued, "I ascertained that Colonel Beckley, with a few companies of a partly organized regiment of cavalry was a few miles beyond Logan Court House on Island Creek, but the distance being considerable, his way of retreat sure, and his having received information two or three days in advance, I determined not to advance a movement against that force, being satisfied that it would be without results worthy of mention. I started back with my command on the morning of the 22d and reached Camp Piatt by 5 p.m. of that day."[169]

General Duffie summarized, "The country through which I marched my command is rugged, the roads being scarcely passable for wagons in low water, and impracticable even for cavalry in low water; the supply of forage is very limited; very little hay is grown in all that country, and barely corn enough to subsist a part of the inhabitants."[170]

The 45th Battalion had one man taken prisoner by Federals on the expedition; the battalion returned to Logan and continued recruiting efforts and small patrols. It should be noted that one historian warned while Federal reports during this period often mention small skirmishes with "bushwhackers," it is not specific to the 45th Battalion.[171]

The next incident experienced by men of the 45th Battalion was less ambiguous, as on December 10, 1863 Captain John S. Witcher of the 3rd West Virginia Cavalry led a detachment of fifty men on a scout covering 150 miles in three days through Logan, Wayne and Boone Counties. Captain Witcher reported capturing an unknown number of soldiers from the 45th Battalion Virginia Infantry, although he also reported capturing men from the Virginia State Line, which was disbanded in March 1863.[172] Because they had moved away from the Tug River Valley, many of the men in Colonel Beckley's battalion became demoralized about leaving their families alone with frequent raids on Southern homes in the region. As a result, desertions, which had started to escalate in September 1863, were more frequent by December 15, 1861. By December 20, the 45th Battalion returned to Camp Georgia at Tazewell County, Virginia. The 45th Battalion remained in Tazewell County, Virginia through the end of January. Then, it was reassigned to Brigadier General John McCausland's brigade of infantry, along with the 36th Virginia Infantry, 60th Virginia Infantry, and Bryan's Artillery Battery, and was in this brigade until the end of the war. Near the end of January, the brigade established winter quarters near Princeton, West Virginia, and remained there until April 1, 1864.[173]

Word reached the camp of yet another skirmish at Wayne Court House and subsequent retaliation against Southern citizens in the Logan and Wayne areas on January 27, 1864. Most of Company F were from this area, and several members subsequently deserted. Captain John S. Witcher of Company G, 3rd West Virginia Cavalry, attacked a small detachment of thirty to thirty-five men from the 16th Virginia Cavalry, under Captain Hurston Spurlock, near Twelve Pole Creek in Wayne County.[174]

Hurston Spurlock was a popular resident of Wayne County, and a successful merchant prior to the war. He became notorious for harassing Union citizens in the region during the war and was captured in the attack.[175]

By March 1864, roughly ten percent of the 45th Battalion was listed as deserters on muster rolls, although, as noted earlier, Devil Anse was gone by that time, as he was found missing in late 1863, and by February 1, 1864 was listed as a deserter.[176]

Why did Devil Anse Desert?

While the precise reason for Hatfield's taking "French Leave" (Civil War era parlance for desertion) is not mentioned in military records, family tradition alleges that it was because Devil Anse was ordered to lead a firing squad in the execution of his uncle, James G. "Slater Jim" Hatfield, Anse Toler, and Jonathan Morgan of Wyoming County for deserting in the fall of 1863. The three had supposedly asked Devil Anse, who was an officer with potential influence, to intercede with Colonel Alfred M. Beckley regarding their request for leave to return to Logan because Toler's wife was deathly ill.[177]

When the Colonel refused, they left anyway, and arrived just in time for Toler to see his wife before she died. They promptly returned but Colonel Beckley is said to have ordered an immediate court martial, in which they were found guilty and sentenced to be executed by firing squad. Since he had been their advocate, Devil Anse was ordered to command the firing detail; however, according to family tradition, he groused to Colonel Beckley, "…if Toler and Slater Jim had to die, that many more would bite the dust."[178]

Hatfield was said to have then sent a secret message to his uncle, Jim Vance, who was with Colonel Vincent Witcher's cavalry battalion nearby, informing him of the incident and requesting he prepare a horse and saddle for him to elope the next morning.[179]

Historian Otis K. Rice posited a different version in his book, *The Hatfields and McCoys*; his account states it was George Hatfield and Philip Lambert who deserted and that Devil Anse refused to execute them. He also opined that the death of Devil Anse's friend, General John B. Floyd, on August 26, 1863 was another factor, implying that it may have disillusioned Hatfield.[180]

Contextually, if the account of having his home burned out in July 1863 is true, that probably did more to distance him from the "cause" than anything. Otis Rice also noted that on a larger scale, Confederate sympathizers in the Tug River Valley were left in a "precarious" position when West Virginia was admitted into the Union on June 20, 1863 because they were losing political influence and property in government "confiscations" by opposing the new state government.[181]

Author Altina Waller noted that in the absence of other information, many writers have assumed that the mountaineers wanted less military structure and more opportunities to "rob, steal, and plunder." Waller also states that readers should bear in mind that no one ever made such claims against soldiers in the American Revolution, who often deserted to protect their homes or to harvest crops, and that in the case of the Hatfields and McCoys, events at home were a more plausible explanation for their desertion.[182]

Since the Union army had established control over West Virginia and eastern Kentucky by late 1863, men in the 45th Battalion were cognizant of how the tide of the war had turned against them. Many soldiers knew all too well that by remaining in the army away from their homes that their families were in danger.

Considering Devil Anse's strong self-reliance and loyalty to family, it is likely that by late 1863 he and others who deserted had no interest in becoming "martyrs for the lost cause." Possibly the most accurate explanation is given by historian James Prichard, who succinctly states, "Many mountaineers apparently felt that the Confederate government expected them to sacrifice not only their lives for the cause, but their homes and families as well. Quite possibly, Hatfield would have agreed with one Virginia mountaineer who defended his decision to return home with a defiant 'Richmond be damned.'"[183]

This is further evidenced by several other men from his home area deserting in the same period including Devil Anse's brother Elias Hatfield, as well as Ephraim Hatfield and later feudist Selkirk McCoy. Ultimately, what we do know is that Devil Anse left the army and returned home and formed a partisan guerrilla company, although details of his activities during this period are limited, to say the least.[184]

Devil Anse Hatfield.
American Journal of Sociology, 1901.

Devil Anse and other armed men. Public domain.
Devil Anse is on left. Note he is wearing a haversack, a painted canvas bag used in the Civil War to carry rations and personal items. He has cut the strap so short that it rides under his armpit, a common practice of Confederate soldiers in western Virginia. This prevented the haversack from interfering on the march across the rough, mountainous terrain.

4

1864-1865: Partisan Guerrilla

A 45th Battalion Virginia Infantry muster roll of February 1, 1864, indicates Devil Anse was listed as a deserter. After that time, most accounts place Hatfield as the leader of a guerrilla or partisan cavalry company comprised mainly of men who formerly served with him in the 45th Battalion Virginia Infantry. Hatfield once stated in an 1889 interview with the *Wheeling Intelligencer* that he was in an independent company after leaving the 45th Battalion. He disclosed, "I...then recruited a company which was kept in service in Wayne, Cabell, and other border counties of West Virginia and Kentucky." Yet, some oral and family tradition accounts also conflict as to which partisan group he served with.[185]

Taken at face value, Hatfield's own words generally describe his actions after leaving the 45th Battalion, although the lack of military records documenting this period of his military service makes it difficult to discern details of his activities. The same was true for many other independent partisan companies in 1864-1865, however. Since their operations were not officially sanctioned by the Confederate government, most did not bother with making written reports of their activities.[186]

However, two historians and Hatfield family tradition agree that Devil Anse aligned with Wayne County, West Virginia resident William S. "Rebel Bill" Smith's partisan guerrilla organization sometime in late 1863, or winter of 1864 after returning home. Readers are cautioned, however, that while Devil Anse described operating an independent partisan company in Logan and other border counties during his 1889 interview with the *Wheeling Intelligencer*, he did not specifically mention any ties to Smith's Battalion. However, there is evidence of their connection found in a letter Smith wrote to Kentucky Governor Simon B. Buckner on October 12, 1889; therein, he stated that Hatfield had served in his battalion. Also, there are post war court records in Pike County, Kentucky, accusing Hatfield of being present with Rebel Bill Smith during several raids against Unionists in the area. It is also interesting to note that Smith's son, Larkin, married Hatfield's younger sister Emma during the Civil War.[187]

Virgil Carrington Jones, who authored several books on the Civil War, also wrote the 1948 book *The Hatfields and the McCoys*. In spite of rather superfluous and stereotyped accounts of the feudists, he still posits a fairly accurate picture of the partisan guerrillas operating from 1863 through the end of the war in the Tug Valley region: "By late '63, the border warfare...was in full swing, and the hottest part of it was along the Tug and Big Sandy Rivers. There renegade bands of guerrillas were ranging the respective shores on behalf of the North or the South..." Historian James Prichard further points out that the partisans on both sides adhered to the ancient law, "an eye for an eye", noting that usually a raid from one side of the Tug River would soon be followed by one from the other.[188]

Virgil Carrington Jones continued, "These opposing guerrilla bands made it dangerous during the last two years of the war for unidentified Northerner or Southerner to make his way up the Big Sandy or the Tug. The bands organized presumably for home defense, but their activities were not always confined to legitimate undertakings. The spoils they claimed often failed to be in keeping with the rules of warfare."[189]

He further wrote, "Likewise, bullets from their guns occasionally made their way into places where they should not have been, and more rarely into victims for whom they were not intended. The reputation of these fighters was not good, even among their own adherents. But their warfare went on with regular intensity. They fought when the occasion arose, and, whenever the fighting waned, often as not spent their idle moments raising unadulterated hell around some mountain moonshine still."[190]

Jones also asserted that "one of the most feared bands on the West Virginia side toted guns under the leadership of Devil Anse Hatfield. He had fought at the beginning with the militia. In 1862, he enlisted in the regular Confederate army and became a first lieutenant of Company A, Forty-fifth Virginia Infantry. The following year, as a captain, he left the regular service to take up the warfare of an independent in Logan, Pike, Wayne, Cabell and other border counties."[191]

Errors in Devil Anse's service record cited in Jones's account aside, (Hatfield was never a captain during the Civil War and was in Company B) other sources have similarly reported also that Hatfield's partisan guerrilla company were dreaded throughout the area. However, he goes on to relate an anecdotal account of how Hatfield supposedly singlehandedly held off a large body of Union troops for several hours until dark at a place known as the "Devil's Backbone" located in "the wilds of Logan County." This tale appears in several popular feud accounts, although is unsupported by either Union or Confederate military records.[192]

There is another similar version in oral tradition that supposedly occurred sometime during 1888-1889, when Hatfield was said to have held off a group of armed bounty hunters chasing him at the Devil's Backbone for several hours, supposedly "killing them all." At least one author has dismissed the legend altogether, contending that the affair "...never happened."[193]

Obviously, there is much inaccuracy in extant feud literature related to this era of Hatfield's military service, although many sources agree that after deserting the Confederate army, Hatfield was the recognized leader of a large Confederate partisan faction on the Tug River. On the other hand, there is little consistency as to when this era of his service began; accounts vary, but most writers place it during the late 1863 or early 1864 period. Note that some of the same sources have also erroneously claimed the name of Hatfield's partisan outfit was the Logan Wildcats, however.[194]

Considering earlier appraisals of Hatfield's character and evidence that soldiers were beginning to realize the Confederate government expected them to also sacrifice their homes and families if needed, it becomes more doubtful Devil Anse that had any desire to sustain the Southern cause as much as to protect his family. Coleman C. Hatfield's account states that Devil Anse realized the Confederacy was doomed after General Robert E. Lee's loss at Gettysburg July 1-3, 1863, and that his best option to protect his home was to return to the Tug River Valley, acting "independently of the Rebel Army but in general accord with the Confederate war aims."[195]

Historian Jeffrey Weaver rather bluntly indicated that "a great deal has been written about desertion among soldiers from western Virginia, but much of the general perception is incorrect. Desertions from the Confederate ranks usually stemmed more from a desire to protect family and friends, rather than a desire to undermine the Confederate attempt to gain independence."

Weaver further opined, "While elitist Southern society generally felt that the more well-settled, populated areas in Georgia, the Carolinas, and Virginia should be protected, the Appalachian region was quickly given up to Federal domination. The elites usually made disparaging remarks about the inhabitants and the geography, betraying their feelings about their back-woods cousins." Weaver also opined that by deserting his post to return home and disobeying orders of the Confederate hierarchy, Devil Anse became a "local hero."[196]

Another historian asserted that "Tug Valley residents, in choosing the South, were not embracing the idea of Southern nationhood so much as defending their autonomy. The alacrity with which mountaineers deserted the regular army to form guerrilla bands operating in their own region is further proof of the point."[197]

Rebel Bill Smith was the identified leader of a large partisan guerrilla battalion in the Logan area, known as "Smith's Battalion," which had at least five companies, possibly more, of three to four hundred men, many of whom were deserters from the 45th Battalion Virginia Infantry. Smith's Battalion was active in the Tug River Valley area from mid-1863 to the end of the war in 1865. Rebel Bill was "One of the most noted partisans in western Virginia, the Wayne County native hoped to rally the hundreds of Confederate deserters and absentees in the region with the promise of service on the border. Smith hoped to carve out his own 'Confederacy' along the Sandy, as John S. Mosby had done in the Shenandoah Valley."[198]

Smith was initially a member of a volunteer company known as the Fairview Rifle Guards, who some researchers believe were also part of the 167th Regiment Virginia Militia, although unit records do not show Smith on the rolls. Smith is thought to have served with Ferguson at the battle of Barboursville on July 12, 1861, and with the Sandy Rangers under Captain James M. Corns of Wayne County, during the battle of Scary Creek on July 18, 1861. The Sandy Rangers achieved regional notoriety when they saved the Confederate lines in a fierce and daring last minute charge across the bridge, forcing the Federal troops to retreat.

Hatfield family tradition also claims that Devil Anse was present with the Sandy Rangers at Scary Creek, although as discussed in Chapter One, there is no archival evidence to support the notion. Coleman Hatfield wrote that Devil Anse later accused Smith of being a coward. He supposedly claimed that Rebel Bill ran from their ranks to take cover along the creek bank so quickly that his "coat tails stood out straight." On the other hand, that story emerged during the feud era after Devil Anse learned that Smith had offered his services to Kentucky Governor Simon B. Buckner to bring him to justice. Military records also fail to show Hatfield was ever part of the Sandy Rangers, raising more doubts that it was factual.[199]

Smith later enlisted as a private in Company K, 8th Virginia Cavalry on or about January 15, 1862, when the Sandy Rangers consolidated with the Fairview Rifle Guards. He served in that unit until July 1862, when he was detailed to Brigadier General John B. Floyd in the Virginia State Line, although the purpose is unclear in his service records. He remained with Floyd only briefly, however, as in August 1862 he raised a company that became Company D, 2nd Battalion Kentucky Mounted Rifles. He obtained an officer's commission, and resigned on January 24, 1864, "by reason of being in command of a battalion currently raised on the border of N.W. Va. in the counties of Wayne, Logan & C."[200]

While the specific activities of Smith's Battalion are generally elusive, and there are no records indicating specific ranks of the leaders, five men leading companies in the battalion were identified as Melvin B. Lawson and John C. Chafin of Logan County, Benjamin J. Smith of Wayne County, Julius Williamson and John H. Livingston of Pike and Lawrence Counties, Kentucky, respectively. At least part of Hatfield's objective with his company of irregulars was to protect Southern citizens in Logan County from Unionist neighbors. They could not, however, prevent Union military raids or home guard operations in the

William S. "Rebel Bill" Smith.
Courtesy of Evelyn B. Massie.

region, particularly against well armed Federal cavalry units scouting through the vicinity.[201]

Shortly after Smith organized his battalion, he petitioned Confederate authorities in Richmond to recognize his unit as partisan rangers claiming to have raised nearly 600 men; however, the law authorizing such groups was repealed in early 1864 and Smith never received the independent command status he coveted. This also meant the Confederate government would not pay, or supply nor take responsibility for his battalion. Smith brought his case to Brigadier General John Hunt Morgan, who agreed to have his battalion brought under his command and petitioned Confederate authorities in Richmond on his behalf early in 1864. Major General James Longstreet commanded Confederate forces in that region during this part of the war, and he also agreed and granted authority for Morgan to muster the battalion into service with him.

However, before Morgan could do so, Confederate Adjutant General and Inspector General Samuel Cooper interceded. Cooper was not a supporter of guerrilla tactics and declined Longstreet's request to acquire the battalion on grounds that partisan battalions tended to produced dissatisfaction and restlessness among the soldiers. Smith persisted and was repeatedly denied recognition from Confederate authorities.[202]

The *Ironton Register* newspaper reported on March 24, 1864, that Rebel Bill Smith had recently executed a mission into Catlettsburg, Kentucky in Boyd County and raided a U.S. Government horse farm. The newspaper retracted the story shortly afterward, stating in a March 30, 1864 edition that the previous account might have originated from another report indicating Smith had raided a dry goods store in Peach Orchard, Kentucky, owned by Colonel John Dils, who commanded the 39th Kentucky Mounted Infantry, the previous week. The article indicated "Bill Smith, the notorious guerrilla and horse thief visited Boyd County, Ky.; about 10 miles from the mouth of Big Sandy on last Wednesday after committing other depredations, took with him 13 of the best horses of the community."[203]

Smith's raiders reportedly helped themselves to over $7,000 worth of Colonel Dill's supplies and ransacked two other local supply stores. Their plunder was valued at an additional $700. Hatfield's company is presumed to have been with Smith on this raid, which although speculative, he would have doubtlessly enjoyed repaying at least part of the hardships said to have been caused by Dils' men burning his home in 1863.[204]

Another incident occurring in Wyoming County during mid-August 1864 reportedly involved Hatfield and numerous other former members of Beckley's Battalion. Hatfield's company, together with former comrades from Company C, 45th Battalion Virginia Infantry led by Captain Russell Cook, engaged a small squad of Union home guards under Captain Charles Stewart near Matheny Chapel. There, the guerrillas and Confederates significantly outnumbered the Unionists; once discovered, Hatfield et al. are said to have hastily attacked the home guardsmen "with yells and shooting" while hidden in a nearby wooded area. Once in a better position, both sides maintained a great deal of firing, and some of the home guard returned the yells.[205]

Recognizing he was outgunned, Captain Stewart retreated across the Laurel Fork and sought safety in the heavily wooded hillside across the stream. In the process, they encountered a small group of civilians, who were apparently Union men, playing cards in a wooded camp site. When they heard the commotion, the gamblers jumped up and leaped off the cliff, and ran down the hill toward Staggerweed, a small village nearby.

One of the men was shot in the foot and in the body by Confederates trying to escape and was left behind. Captain Stewart decided the woods were full of Confederates and crossed the mountain over to Simmons Fork. The affair caused more tensions between Wyoming County's Unionists and Southern supporters; Captain Stewart was afterward ambushed, and was severely wounded, but not killed, coming out of his own home by one of the Southern leaders in the county. He recovered and returned to duty in the home guards.[206]

Although possibly apocryphal, there is also a story of one Union soldier involved in the skirmish, who was a former member of the 45th Battalion Virginia Infantry, named Harry Cook. He was known as something of an intellectual for his habit of studying philosophy books in camp. After his departure from the regiment to enlist in the Union army, Cook became a target among local Confederates and guerrilla outfits, including Hatfield's company, who were supposedly familiar with him. Cook's intellectual pursuits proved more than an academic fancy in camp, however, as during the skirmish, one of the Confederates fired at his back while on retreat, and a musket ball struck a philosophy book he had tucked away in his knapsack, the thickness of which likely prevented his death. He later joked that his intellectual pursuits had saved his life.[207]

In late September 1864, Union Cavalry from eastern Kentucky launched a large-scale raid on Saltville; this left the region with only minimal Union troops. Rebel Bill and his battalion took advantage of the opportunity, striking a small Union outpost located at Peach Orchard, Kentucky in Lawrence County near Louisa on or about October 12, 1864. There was a large supply warehouse and several well-stocked stores there, including the one owned by Colonel John Dils of the 39th Kentucky Mounted Infantry. Recall that Smith and Hatfield earlier raided Dils' store in March 1864.

This time the loot was $3,500 worth of goods taken, primarily boots, hats, and clothing from not only Dils, but also a large warehouse, owned by prominent Pike County Unionist Thomas J. Sowards, who previously served as a captain commanding a company in Dils' regiment; it was torched after Smith and Hatfield et al. plundered it.[208]

Later there were several court cases in Pike and Lawrence County, Kentucky, filed against Confederates who had participated in the raids, including Devil Anse, Elias, and Ellison Hatfield, as well as Johnson McCoy. Interestingly, another party involved in the litigation was Jacob Cline, Jr., the Unionist son of a major antagonist and arch enemy of Devil Anse's during the feud years. However, while Cline had earlier served in the 39th Kentucky under Colonel Dils, and later also reenlisted in 1865, he was forced under threat of death to accompany them on the October 12, 1864 raid, according to Devil Anse's testimony on behalf of Cline Jr. in 1866.[209]

The famous feud was not the only time Devil Anse was accused of killing someone, however. Detective Dan Cunningham wrote in his memoirs that sometime prior to August 1864, Pike County residents Asbury Hurley and his sixteen-year-old son, who served in the 39th Kentucky Infantry, were home on leave. They had recently been deemed by Devil Anse and his company as "bushwhackers" for killing one of their men. According to the narrative, they "soon learned that Anse and his gang were after them" and hid-out in a nearby cave.

Once Hatfield found them, he was said to have promised to treat them as prisoners of war to entice them to surrender, and then took them out to a large, flat rock, tied side by side, and executed them both. Each had deserted the Union army in August 1864, after learning that United States Colored Troops were to be stationed alongside them. Bear in mind, however, that Cunningham's memoirs are thought by several historians suspect for bias due not only to his pursuit of Devil Anse as a detective during the feud years, but also because his father and brother served in the Union army.[210]

Despite a lack of formal recognition by the Confederate government, Smith's battalion continued to effectively harass Union troops stationed in eastern Kentucky throughout the fall of 1864. In late September, Smith captured several privates, a sergeant major and lieutenant colonel from the 68th Kentucky Enrolled Militia (Union) and stole a horse and a mule from that regiment in a hastily planned raid also in September 1864.[211]

Colonel Thomas McKinster, who commanded the 68th Kentucky Militia, recalled that Smith's men so terrified one of the African American regiments serving in Eastern Kentucky that they refused to go out on patrol when the battalion was nearby. Smith's men were said to have recently taken several horses and robbed ten or twelve African American soldiers in an otherwise undocumented encounter that spurred the soldier's dread.[212]

Captain Benjamin R. Hayley led a Union home guard company in Wayne County, who was captured by Smith in a skirmish on or about September 15, 1864. Captain Hayley wrote to West Virginia Governor Arthur Boreman for help, complaining that his men were constantly harassed by Smith's battalion. Hayley informed Boreman that he and seven of his men were surrounded by Smith's partisans, and "We were all gobbled up with our arms and accoutrements making in all Seventeen guns…" Hayley further noted of Smith, "his gang in our midst…gives us much trouble and fatigue." Haley's fears soon piqued when Smith's men captured him along with seventeen others and sent them to a Confederate prison.[213]

A resident of Wayne County observed that citizens there had lately become "very much annoyed" with Hayley's company, because while "a part of that company had some respect for the rights of citizens, others had no such respect, and made abuse of their power as armed men merely. It is said that the commander and a portion of the men were drunk a good part of the time, and threatened to kill citizens who would not approve of their drunken (illegible), or against whom they have conjured up feelings of bitterness for some imaginary wrong."[214]

In early November 1864, Smith's battalion became affiliated with Colonel Vincent Witcher's 34th Battalion Virginia Cavalry. On or about November 5, 1864, they conducted a raid on the Union garrison at Peach Orchard. During this period, Smith and Witcher's battalions also became affiliated with Captain Ezekial Counts' battalion. Counts was often referred to by locals as "Devil Zeke."[215]

While it is unknown whether Hatfield's company was present, Witcher's battalion had recently also executed another raid on the Union garrison at the village of Barboursville in Cabell County during late October, as reported in the November 3, 1864 Weekly Register. Smith reportedly had around 500 men and "made a dash" into the village, "burning the government stables there, robbed the only store in the place, and carried off several of the citizens."[216]

The *Weekly Register* also indicated that "whenever these scoundrels came across a citizen they demanded 'his greenbacks' under penalty of death if they did not comply with the demand. They also stole several horses. Wayne and Cabell Counties are now completely overrun with these cutthroats and robbers. Something ought to be done to protect the people of those counties." After a sharp skirmish, the partisans burned government stables, and retreated toward Logan.[217]

On November 5, 1864, Smith and Hatfield were said to have

accompanied Witcher's battalion to Buffalo Shoals where they captured and burned two U.S. Steamers, the *Barnum* and the *Fawn*. According to the *Louisville Daily Journal*, Federal losses were reportedly several small arms destroyed, two killed and five prisoners, although several other Union soldiers escaped because they could not cross the Sandy River into Kentucky. Witcher also reported destroying a large supply of military stores the same day at Mellonsburg, including the cooking utensils for an entire brigade, and drove Federal cavalry back to their fortifications at Louisa.[218]

Another account from the *Louisville Daily Journal* has Smith and Hatfield, along with "Devil Zeke" Ezekial R. Counts, leading a band of around 100 men into the Rockcastle precinct of Lawrence County, Kentucky on November 8, 1864 intending to disrupt the election. Ezekial Counts forced election officials to allow thirty men to cast votes in favor of George B. McClellan, the former major general who ran against Abraham Lincoln. Some of the partisans supposedly told the election officials they voted for Lincoln, because they "thought they could whip him, but did not know about whipping McClellan."Twenty-eight of the men were indicted after the war on charges of Fraudulent Voting in Lawrence County Circuit Court, with Devil Anse's name at the top of the list.[219]

Also, near mid-November 1864, Hatfield's company is said to have participated in another raid with Smith along the Tug River near Louisa, Kentucky, and attempted to engage a group of Union home guards in a small skirmish. However, the Unionists tried to avoid a fight, which only served to antagonize Rebel Bill. As one man tried to surrender, begging Smith not to shoot him, he struck him on the head with his pistol and scolded him, calling him a coward.[220]

One writer noted that Smith had earlier promised that any prisoners taken by his men would be allowed to remain at home, so long as they took an oath not to take up arms against the Confederacy again. He also perceived that Smith's men had a very embittered attitude toward anyone connected with the "...State of West Virginia, militarily or otherwise." Again, the reader is cautioned that while some authors believe Hatfield was present on these operations, there is no known documentation of such.[221]

Witcher's command moved into Wyoming County on November 16, 1864, but Smith stayed in Logan. By February 1865, the war was ending, and apparently Smith's operations were beginning to deescalate. Major Edgar Blundon of the 7th West Virginia Cavalry reported on March 5, 1865 what is thought to be among the last activities of Smith's Battalion documented in the war. Blundon wrote, "There is but one organized band of guerrillas, consisting of Bill Smith and fifteen or twenty men, in Wayne or Logan Counties, and no organization in Mason, Cabell or Putnam."[222]

He continued,

> "The depredations committed by them are comparatively few contrasted with the past. No boats, either steam or trading boats, have been interfered with, nor has navigation been stopped for a moment on account of guerillas. There are a few deserters from United States and rebel armies who have gone into the mountains to evade pursuit and capture who sometimes rob individuals of money and clothing without regard to political status. The men of this detachment are thoroughly acquainted with every road, stream or path in this section, many of them having been raised in the counties names, which has rendered our efforts successful in capturing all the notorious rebels in this section except Smith, and we are sanguine that we shall soon rid the country of him and squad."

Otherwise, Hatfield's partisan activities during the winter of 1864-1865 remain largely ambiguous, although he and his wife Levicy conceived another child, who was born the following summer.[223]

As the war gradually ended in the border territories of Kentucky and West Virginia, Devil Anse traveled to Charleston where he took the Oath of Allegiance on May 11, 1865. Those taking the Oath received the same parole conditions as Lieutenant General Ulysses S. Grant gave to General Robert E. Lee's Army of Northern Virginia at Appomattox on April 9, 1865.

One historian opined that "When the war ended, Hatfield's band lay down their arms and reluctantly accepted the Unionist order. As such, some recent scholars have argued that because Devil Anse appears to have accepted the restoration of Federal order, that the war had nothing to do with the famous feud. This assessment, however, is not entirely correct. Some long-simmering hatreds developed between the Hatfields and the Cline family, who were supporters of the McCoys, Pike County residents, and ardent Republicans in the postwar period."[224]

Well armed and mounted Devil Anse Hatfield.
West Virginia State Archives.

5

1865: Murder of Asa Harmon McCoy

One of the last known incidents of the Civil War associated with Devil Anse Hatfield occurred at Caney Branch Hollow in Pike County, Kentucky, on January 7, 1865. Although his involvement remains unproven, many researchers and historians believe this was a primary cause of the Hatfield and McCoy feud. On that date, thirty-seven-year-old Asa Harmon McCoy, the younger brother of Randall McCoy, was murdered. McCoy resided in Lawrence County, Kentucky, before the war and was known for strong loyalty to the Union, although because he also had slaves, he was something of a paradox.[225]

Asa Harmon initially served in a Union home guard company led by Captain Uriah Runyon at Peter Creek, in Pike County, Kentucky. Just three days after enlisting in that unit on February 13, 1862, he suffered a gunshot wound to the chest in a small skirmish near the Big Sandy River. Rumors flurried that it was Devil Anse Hatfield who had shot him. Records show that McCoy was in fact wounded; however, only family and oral tradition supports the notion that it was Devil Anse who shot him, and he never mentioned it in printed sources.[226]

Capt Uriah Runnions Roll

1 W. R. Johnson
2 Peyton Johnson
3 Daniel Mounts
4 Adam Runnions
5 Har. Runnions
6 Peter Cline
7 Harrison Mounts
8 Asbury Runnions
9 Daniel Noe
10 Isaac Noe
11 Charles Mounts
12 Chas. W. Mounts
13 Rich. Daniels
14 Wed. White
15 Daniel White
16 Ed. White
17 Jos. White
18 Peres White
19 William Hagerman
20 Hiram Gyles
21 Allen Stafford
22 Emly Mounts
23 Ely. Mounts Sr
24 William Daniels
25 Jacob Cline
26 Elisha Stafford
27 Amos Wallis
28 Enoch Cassady
29 E. Mounts Jr.

30 M. Daniels
31 Geo. Wolford
32 N. Hare
33 M. Mounts
34 Wm. Mounts
35 Wm Robnet
36 John Steele
37 Wm Christian
38 Lewis Daniel
39 Asbury Mounts
40 Wm Mounts Sr
41 Wm. R. Cravens
42 John McCoy
43 Daniel Daniels
44 Pleasant McCoy
45 Elias Sansom
46 Andrew Noe
47 Ferrell Stafford
48 J. H. Robnett
49 Asa. Wilson
50 Asa H. McCoy
51 M. Mounts Sr
52 A. Runnions Sr

Captain Uriah Runyon's Union Home Guard Company Muster Roll, 1861, showing Asa Harmon McCoy as a member (3rd from bottom on right hand column, #50). West Virginia State Archives. Used with permission.

After being wounded, Asa Harmon was taken to his home, a farm in Pikeville, Kentucky, to recover; however, troops from the Virginia State Line under Brigadier General John B. Floyd, eventually discovered his whereabouts. Early on the morning of December 5, 1862, they surrounded his home as he was "laying wounded" and captured him. It is unknown whether Devil Anse was involved or not, but he was an officer in the Virginia State Line during this period, and they were in the Pikeville area during December 1862. McCoy was then imprisoned for approximately three to four months at Richmond, Virginia.[227]

On April 7, 1863 he was admitted to an army hospital, and the surgeon there identified him as a member of Captain Cline's Company, 5th Kentucky Volunteer Infantry on that date. Another document of the same date states that he told the doctor he did not know which company or regiment to which he belonged and had never mustered into service.

However, McCoy's name does not appear in service records or other records of the 5th Kentucky Volunteer Infantry. The surgeon wrote that the musket ball striking him two months prior had passed between the "uniform cartilage of the fifth and seventh ribs" that caused him to "spit up" a great deal of fluid and described his condition as "feeble from the effect of so severe an injury and suffering he is exhausted."[228]

As a result, the surgeon deemed him unfit for continued service, and recommended a discharge. However, McCoy eventually recovered, and on October 20, 1863, enlisted in Company E, 45th Kentucky Mounted Infantry for twelve months service at Ashland, Kentucky. Service records show him present on November 30, 1863 when the regiment was involved in a small action at Salyersville, Kentucky, and several operations against guerrillas. However, on or about May 5, 1864, McCoy broke his right leg while thrown from a buggy and was admitted to the Army General Hospital at Lexington, Kentucky.[229]

McCoy was with his regiment again on July 1, 1864, and while likely still recovering, is shown present during operations against guerrillas during August 1864, and the large Union expedition into southwestern Virginia during September – October 1864. Once his term of service ended, he was discharged on December 24, 1864. Thirteen days later, Asa Harmon McCoy was murdered.

Some accounts of the incident posit that shortly after Asa Harmon's discharge, Devil Anse and Jim Vance had threatened to pay him a visit for his role in several raids on Southern citizens. No one was ever indicted for the murder, but initially Devil Anse took the blame. His uncle Jim Vance was also accused of killing McCoy; a version of local tradition claimed that Asa Harmon had mortally wounded Vance's brother, Robert, who served in the Virginia State Line, during a wartime skirmish near Little War Creek. Devil Anse was absolved by an alibi that he was home sick with his wife on the day the murder occurred.[230]

Although mainly rooted in oral and family tradition, there were several incidents said to have caused tensions between Devil Anse and Asa Harmon McCoy prior to his murder in 1865. According to family tradition cited in Coleman Hatfield's *Tale of the Devil*, early in the Civil War Hatfield and some other men from Virginia were caught in the Peter Creek area of Kentucky and accused of spying on the home guards by their leader, Captain William "Yankee Bill" Francis.[231]

Francis was said to have ordered Asa Harmon McCoy, who was in Captain Runyon's company, to fight Devil Anse as punishment. Hatfield got the best of the scrap, but his pride was injured according to his mother, and he decided to enlist and fight against the Unionists. However, other evidence presented in Chapter One indicates Devil Anse was already a member of the Virginia Militia in 1861. With evidence limited to oral tradition, we are left to speculation as to whether these events could explain the supposed tension between Devil Anse and Asa Harmon McCoy.[232]

Also, during fall of 1862, Asa McCoy supposedly took one of his slaves identified only as "Pete" along on a raid led by home guard Captain William "Yankee Bill" Francis, on the home of Moses C. Cline, a friend of Devil Anse and a strong Confederate supporter. Known as "Mose," during the raid he was shot while attempting to stop them from taking off his livestock; Francis's home guards were generally notorious for brutality and violent robberies against Southern citizens. It is unknown which of the men shot and killed Moses C. Cline during the attack, but Devil Anse, believing the wound was fatal, later supposedly promised revenge on Yankee Bill, Asa Harmon and Pete. Some authors

Asa Harmon McCoy.
West Virginia State Archives.

suggest that Devil Anse and his later nemesis during the feud, Randall McCoy, participated in the capture and killing of Captain Francis after Moses C. Cline's murder, but there is no record of it beyond oral tradition.[233]

The alleged tension between Asa Harmon McCoy and Devil Anse was not limited to the shooting of Moses C. Cline or an early war altercation between them; however, Hatfield was also involved in several raids against other Unionists in Pike County during the war. If we believe what detective Dan Cunningham wrote, Devil Anse murdered several Union men on the raids. However, historian James Prichard rightfully points out that most, if not all were lawful combatants;

Cunningham failed to "...add that virtually all the alleged victims were home guards, including Capt. Bill Francis' son James. M., his son-in-law John Charles, Asa Harmon McCoy and his brother-in-law, William Trigg Cline... Numerous post war lawsuits filed in Pike County name members of Francis's or Runyon's Home Guards as alleged participants in the plundering of Southern men in Pike and Logan Counties."[234]

While accounts vary and often conflict, there was still an obvious animosity between local Unionists such as Asa Harmon McCoy and Southern supporters like Devil Anse; particularly since military documents indicate Hatfield served in the Virginia State Line during 1862 and was in the Logan-Pikeville area when many patrols, scouting operations, and small skirmishes and raids against Union home guards occurred.[235]

Despite Dan Cunningham's accusations and various family and oral traditions saying otherwise, it is interesting to note that in an interview with the *Bluefield Daily Telegraph* on October 22, 1920, just shortly before his death, Devil Anse denied ever killing anyone. Various accounts suggest that he may have killed as many as fifteen men during the war, robbing several others, as well as plundering many houses and farms while engaged in guerrilla operations. During the feud era, he was obviously accused of several murders, but there was never enough evidence to bring conviction in court, only family tradition.[236]

Despite many researchers' belief that Asa Harmon's murder played a causative role in the later feud, there are also some who question it. Some writers contend that McCoy was an outcast in his own family and community because he served in the Union army. However, the Peter Creek area in Pike County was home to a fairly large Union contingent, and two companies of Union home guards were organized from residents there during the war. On the other hand, his brother Randall McCoy served in the Confederate Army, and was incarcerated in a Union prison from 1863-1865. Also, his cousins Asa Peter McCoy and John McCoy, along with two of his sisters, married into the Cline family who were pro-Union, and were involved in small skirmishes against Ellison Hatfield in 1863. One of Devil Anse's relatives, "Deacon Anse" also fought for the Union.[237]

Yet, some oral tradition holds that McCoy's death was to avenge the killing of Devil Anse's friend Moses C. Cline, or in response to his actions serving in the Union home guards. McCoy family tradition denied it was a personal killing, but rather viewed it as an act of war, and therefore did not violate their sense of family honor. Later sources indicate Hatfield and other feudists continued to view the Pikeville area as "hostile territory" long after the war, and given the number of indictments for him and other Hatfields during the Reconstruction era, we can be certain Devil Anse evidenced a contempt for Kentucky law, although lack evidence to prove he was part of any killings. These indictments included his capturing three of Randolph's sons from Kentucky law enforcement officers by force and executing them in West Virginia following the 1882 election day murder of his brother, Ellison Hatfield.[238]

Ultimately, the McCoy family in fact did nothing to exact revenge for Asa Harmon's murder. Some accounts posit they simply shrugged off Asa's death, saying that he brought it on himself for supporting the Union. Other accounts suggest that since the family patriarch, Randall McCoy, was still in a Union prison until July 1865, they had no one to lead them in seeking revenge. Historian Altina Waller argued that the killing could not have caused the later feud because thirteen years lapsed before the onset of feud violence. While that is not unreasonable, there were numerous Confederate partisans operating in the region at the time of his death, and some family members may have been too frightened to act, even after the war ended. It is also possible they would have been perceived as Union supporters for doing so, which would be a possible deterrent, but since there was a large contingent of Union supporters in the area, that may not be the case.[239]

Another plausible factor accounting for the delay in feud violence, was that most of the later feudists were children under age twelve years at the time Asa Harmon McCoy was murdered. Although the McCoy family had an earlier start, and as a result had more "fighting age sons" than the Hatfields, a thirteen year lapse is partly explicable by the amount of time it took for young future feudists to reach an age affording enough maturity to participate.[240]

In other words, being very young during the war, or born afterward, those feudists, after listening to family accounts of the war for over a decade, were no doubt influenced by those stories, as well as growing up during Reconstruction and witnessing the tension among former Confederates and Unionists. There were decidedly residual tensions in the region that continued to influence inhabitants of the eastern Kentucky and West Virginia border areas for decades after the Civil War. At the end of the day, there are varying accounts and many discrepancies in feud writings dealing with the murder of Asa Harmon McCoy; the question of whether Devil Anse was involved is doubtful but remains open to debate.[241]

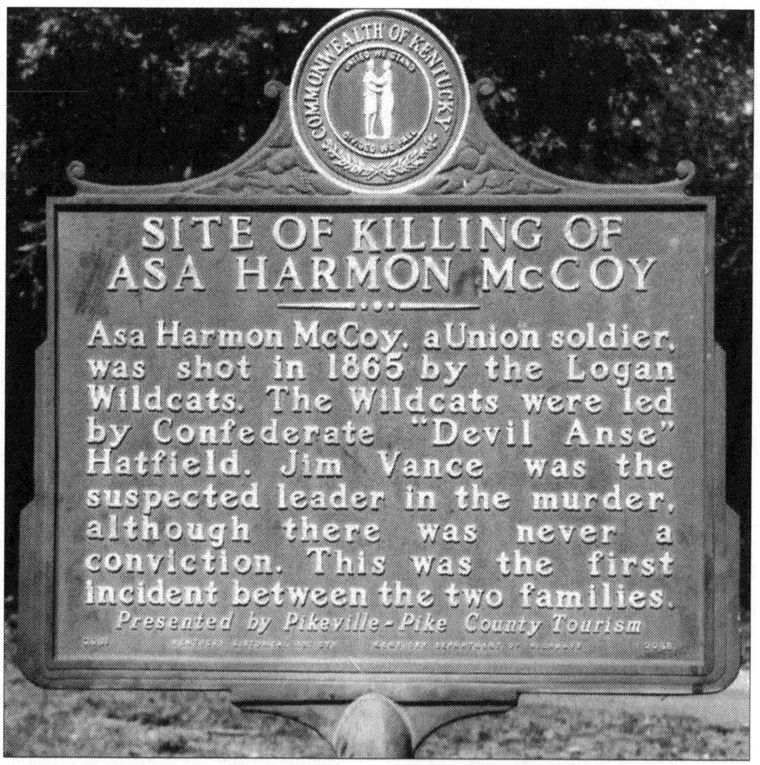

Historical marker, Blackberry, Pike County, Kentucky.
Photo by Heather New, Bloody Mingo Tours.

Location where Asa Harmon McCoy was killed.
Photo by Heather New, Bloody Mingo Tours.

6

Legacy Theory: Did the Civil War Play a Causal Role in the Famous Feud?

The question of whether the Civil War contributed to later feud violence among the Hatfield and McCoy families is herein referred to as the "Legacy Theory." Like other parts of the feud literature, this issue has become a source of contention among scholars and other researchers. One author stated in 1948, "There is general disagreement too, over the factors that led to the feud. Even the feudists themselves have never agreed upon this point." Historian Otis Rice also stated, "At the outset, it must be recognized that the origins of the feud were complex and cannot be identified with one particular event." Despite this, much evidence points toward wartime tensions as a root cause of the famous feud. Historian John D. Preston correctly summarized, "The end of the war did not mean the end of violence" for the Big Sandy region of eastern Kentucky and West Virginia.[242]

It is important to grasp that contextually, most Civil War veterans residing in West Virginia and eastern Kentucky bore long term resentments, harboring a great deal of animosity toward one another for years after the conflict ended, particularly in regions formerly aligned with the Confederacy. One researcher recently suggested that Confederate veterans were struggling to re-integrate into society under the newly formed West Virginia government, because it failed to address the long-standing ideological differences that led residents of former western Virginia to choose sides in the first place. This was because such efforts were predicated on reconciliationist sentiments rather than mutually agreed upon support for new economic and industrial developments in the region.[243]

In other words, the government and partnering industrialists who were set to make large sums of money in the region from the labor force simply encouraged veterans to "forget" the war and focus on mutually beneficial economic developments, when in reality most were still holding grudges and quite divided ideologically. Compared to other parts of the South, there were relatively few former slaves in the region who would have been considered competition for work and wages; hence, that is likely a limited factor in terms of economic causes. Conditions generally became so unsettled along the Kentucky-West Virginia border for many years after the Civil War ended, however, that Federal troops were sent to Logan and Wayne counties in 1867 and remained until 1869.[244]

For example, on March 23, 1866, a Wayne County, West Virginia Unionist appealed to the governor for troops, claiming that timber crews comprised of ex-Rebels from Pike County, Kentucky, and neighboring Logan County, West Virginia, were terrorizing residents in areas near the mouth of the Tug River. The "die-hard Rebels" harassed Union leaning residents by cheering for "Jeff Davis, cursing the Federal government, and there were even incidents of them assaulting Union veterans and the local sheriff. Some wealthy former Confederates, however, would gladly "let bygones be bygones" and become partners in the economic redevelopment of the region in exchange for restored citizenship after the war. This was not the case for many less well-off Confederate veterans. Because of this, many reconciliationist officials found "a distinction between the leaders and common soldiers of the Confederacy and wished to shape the disfranchising amendment to target wealthy and influential ex-Confederates."[245]

Author Altina Waller sought to dismiss the notion that the Civil War played a causative role in the feud, noting that the "…Civil War 'legacy' for the feud, was less a specific incident than the general condition of chaos bequeathed by the war." While there was indeed unrest in the region during the post-war era, that alone is insufficient to explain the onset of feud violence. Waller, who makes a strong argument for the causal role economic factors played in later feud violence, however, also contended that was the primary or root cause. Many accounts of post-war fratricidal violence in the region contradict the notion that it was purely economically motivated. This is further evidenced by the general failure of post-war economic programs on the part of the government and businesses to reconcile the cultural residuals of the Civil War. As discussed in Chapter Five, there are other factors which better account for the onset of feud violence.[246]

Thus, the Civil War remained a contested memory for decades in eastern Kentucky and West Virginia well into the twentieth century. While it is true to a degree that the strong sectionalist feelings and animosities that had led to the war in western Virginia were somewhat mitigated during the Reconstruction era by the recognized potential for economic growth, the Civil War legacy left a strong impact on both economic and sociological development of the new state. This was particularly true in the western areas such as Cabell and Logan Counties, where there were especially large numbers of Confederate veterans. One researcher recently described how in Cabell County, "a new war was beginning in the political halls of state and local governments."[247]

Some historians have also discouraged the notion that Civil War tensions were a cause of the feud because there is evidence Randall McCoy served in the same unit as Devil Anse. While it seems clear that North-South tensions were not a factor in the relationship between the two patriarchs, historian Jeffrey Weaver points out that the notion that the war had nothing to do with the feud is "not entirely correct." He wrote, "Some long simmering hatreds developed between the Hatfields and the Cline family, who were supporters of the McCoys, Pike County residents, and ardent Republicans in the postwar period."[248]

Weaver noted also that the Logan County of 1861 was "far different" than the one in 1866, particularly since West Virginia obtained statehood in 1863 and the new state government was dominated by Republicans, who "imposed a governmental model based on New England municipalities." As most Logan County residents had supported the Confederacy, Weaver asserts that many citizens were as a result deprived of their traditional roles in the community during Reconstruction.

As such, they harbored a deep seated resentment and hostility toward those formerly aligned with the Union during the war, whom they blamed for their political plight. On the other hand, while Confederate veterans who had not taken the Oath of Allegiance were not allowed to vote during those years, many simply lied and did it anyway, because "no one was willing or able to prevent it." Hence, the notion that since Randall McCoy and Devil Anse appeared to have served together in the Confederate army does not negate a link between sectionalist tensions and feud violence.[249]

Historian John D. Preston makes a compelling case connecting the Civil War to the numerous post-war feuds in the Big Sandy region. He opined,

> "The legacy of wartime bitterness helped to spawn the virulent mountain feuds. Eastern Kentuckians had long been used to settling their differences with little recourse to the law. The war gave free rein to this lawlessness by allowing soldiers for the first time to kill and steal with little fear of prosecution or recrimination, and thereby reinforced the notion of personal vengeance for private wrongs. When the law entered into these matters by interfering with the mountaineer's right to avenge himself or his family, the result was the banding together of many members of the extended family for protection.
>
> This attitude stayed in effect after the immediate post-war prosecution period and surfaced in the infamous mountain feuds. Neither local law enforcement officials nor the state

> government were able to quell these feuds for years. It was not until the second decade of the twentieth century that the feuding was permanently stopped. Only when the coal magnates entered Eastern Kentucky and demanded that the state restore a measure of law and order did the fifty-year extension of the Civil War known as feuding finally come to an end."[250]

Decidedly, there were numerous raids, robberies and deaths perpetrated by Union and Confederate soldiers as well as home guards, partisan guerrillas throughout the Tug Valley region during the Civil War, many of whom were later feudists or their closest supporters. There are stark similarities between those vicious wartime guerrilla tactics and the violent executions, ambuscades and raids on family homes later employed during the feud that reveal an indelible link between wartime hostilities and later feud violence in the Big Sandy region.

Historian John D. Preston further wrote, "The fundamental cause of the feuds lay in family relationships, but the activating factor was the series of conditions obtained in the Civil War. The infamous Hatfield-McCoy feud, for example, had its roots in the war. There is no record of differences between the families before the war." There were multiple incidents of targeted fratricidal violence during post-war years along the eastern Kentucky-West Virginia border with roots in wartime events.

One such example occurred in Lawrence County, Kentucky, after the war ended in 1865. Two brothers and former Union soldiers, Hugh Boggs and James Boggs, were murdered by former Confederate John L. Sparks as vengeance for their role in raids against Southern families during the war. Sparks fled to Wise County, Virginia afterward, but some years later, Jesse Boggs, the brother of the two deceased Union soldiers, who was also ironically a former Confederate soldier, found Sparks and exacted his own vengeance, shooting, but not killing him.[251]

Other instances of wartime violence bear a more specific link to the Hatfield-McCoy feud. For example, the 1863 raid on Devil Anse's home is similar to the attack perpetrated on Randall McCoy's home during the feud. Also, the wartime murder of Asa Harmon McCoy similarly bears resemblances to the later capture and execution of the

McCoy brothers. In this context, the wartime experiences of later feudists doubtlessly had an effect on their later willingness to employ targeted, fratricidal violence against their antagonists during the feud era.

Another problem in the Feud literature related to objections that the Civil War had a causal role in the feud, is that it generally fails to account for well-known and common psychological effects of war on veterans, including prisoners of war, which is heavily documented in modern behavioral science research. The reader should understand this is contextual, and does not imply the feudists suffered from mental disorders. Yet, it is well known that combat veterans tend to experience many difficulties readjusting to civilian life, which often includes difficulty maintaining effective family, work and social relationships, with frequent accounts of veterans suffering from intense anger, depression and posttraumatic stress disorder, among other problems.[252]

While modern behavioral science studies were obviously not conducted on Civil War veterans per se, those data do in fact generalize to a multigenerational context. In other words, many modern studies have demonstrated striking similarities in the psychological problems experienced by veterans of World War II, Korea, Vietnam, various Cold War operations, the first Gulf War, and the more recent Iraq-Afghanistan wars, despite there being several years difference in when those wars occurred. Simply put, that literature reveals striking similarities in the psychological effects of war on veterans regardless of which war era they served in, including problems with violence and aggressive behavior after serving in combat.

This is not to suggest that all veterans suffer from psychological disorders or are prone to violence. However, it is not unreasonable to infer that since most of the feudists were combat veterans (see Tables 1 and 2 in the Appendix), they were equally at risk for a tendency to employ violent guerrilla tactics similar to what they learned during wartime. While the reader is therefore cautioned to avoid stereotyping veterans, the feudists who saw combat were not excluded from the risk of suffering psychological effects of war. As such, attempts to dismiss the Legacy Theory which exclude these factors are incomplete.[253]

Another Myth: McCoys Were All Confederates

One of the more common objections to the notion that the Civil War played a role in causing later feud violence is a traditionally held view that the McCoy feudists were all Confederates, and therefore Devil Anse would not have held resentment toward them. Yet, the McCoy family feudists were not as strongly Confederate as many believe. In fact, among the strongest McCoy supporters during the feud were several former Union foes of Devil Anse who were not immediate family members. Also, among McCoy family members who served in the Confederacy with Devil Anse's various regiments, most were Randall McCoy's extended, not immediate, family.[254]

For example, of the McCoy feudists, Uriah McCoy served under Devil Anse in Company B, 45th Battalion Virginia Infantry. Also, William Johnson, Selkirk, and Andrew McCoy each served in Company E, 45th Battalion Virginia Infantry. However, Andrew enlisted in Company E on September 1, 1863, and deserted on the same date, possibly having joined only to gain the bounty pay. Selkirk and Uriah had also served in Company A, 1st Regiment Virginia State Line during 1862 and 1863. Likewise, (William) Johnson McCoy enlisted in the 45th Battalion in July 1863, but also later deserted, supposedly to ride with "Rebel" Bill Smith's battalion along with Devil Anse.[255]

Further, four McCoy family members, James H., Asa Harmon, Samuel B., and Hiram H. served in Union regiments (Table 2), contradicting the notion that the McCoy family were all Confederates. For example, James H. McCoy served in Company D, 5th Kentucky Cavalry. Two of Randall's brothers, Asa Harmon and Samuel B. McCoy, both served in the Union Army; Asa served in Company E, 45th Kentucky Mounted Infantry, and Samuel was in Company B, 12th Kentucky Cavalry. (Table 2) Hiram McCoy, an extended relative of Randall who later fought in the feud, served in Company K, 3rd Kentucky Cavalry Regiment and was present with Major General William T. Sherman on his famous Atlanta Campaign. Obviously, the McCoy feudists were not exclusively Confederate in their allegiances.[256]

Hiram McCoy's son, Thomas McCoy, enlisted in Company I, 1st Virginia State Line in 1862, and served until it disbanded; he later enlisted in Company B, 45th Battalion Virginia Infantry on May 1, 1863, the same company that Devil Anse served in. Thomas deserted in July 1863 to serve with Rebel Bill Smith in Captain Lawson's company. Wiley McCoy was also a Confederate. He enlisted in Company D, 2nd Battalion Kentucky Mounted Rifles (Johnson's Battalion) on August 26, 1862, and by March 1, 1863, had deserted. He later appears on the only known roster of Rebel Bill Smith's battalion in 1864.[257]

In context of the many violent guerrilla and military raids exercised by both Union and Confederates, the Civil War likely had much to do with deep set resentments among veterans residing in the Tug River Valley during the Reconstruction era and later, in addition to other post-war factors such as the civil lawsuits filed against each other by Devil Anse and Randall McCoy.

Summarily, we are left to ponder what Devil Anse said in the 1889 interview with the *Wheeling Intelligencer*:

> When the war ended we all went home and were good friends, until in 1873 or '74, when a difficulty arose between my cousin, Floyd Hatfield, and Randolph McCoy, who had married sister, over a sow and pigs. A lawsuit followed. McCoy was loser, and accused his brother-in-law of swearing falsely, for which he struck McCoy with a stone. Soon after Stratten was waylaid and killed by Paris and Sam McCoy. His brains were shot out. My brother Ellison prosecuted them for murder. He swore out a warrant for their arrest and asked me to execute it. I refused to do it because the McCoys and I had always been good friends.[258]

It is wise to keep in mind that at the time Hatfield recounted the latter, he was facing Federal charges for selling liquor without paying the taxes, and the feud was ongoing for several years. While Devil Anse was known as an honest, straight-forward man, under those circumstances, (he was sought by bounty hunters wishing to take him to Kentucky, and several McCoys were still planning to kill him if they caught him), he had many reasons to dismiss any lingering sense of hostility toward the McCoys speaking to the media.

The reader should also note that several members of both families denied the Civil War had anything to do with the feud. Hopefully, future research will yield more facts as to what role the Civil War played in the complex and multifaceted chain of events leading to the famous fratricide. For time being we are left to grapple with many uncertainties, but there is reliable evidence suggesting the Legacy Theory remains a valid issue in need of further study.

THE OTHER FEUD

Devil Anse Hatfield and Jim Vance are in the center.
West Virginia State Archives.

7

After the Civil War

By all accounts, the Civil War did not end for Devil Anse Hatfield when he took the Oath of Allegiance. As one example, he was sued in Lawrence County, Kentucky during 1866 related to an incident occurring on a raid while he was affiliated with William S. "Rebel Bill" Smith in October 1864. The plaintiff accused Devil Anse as well as Ellison and Elias, and Johnson McCoy of being party to stealing $3,500 in merchandise from former 39th Kentucky Commander John Dils and Thomas J. Sowards.[259]

Shortly after the war, Hatfield was again indicted in Lawrence County, only this time it was for voter fraud. In November 1864, when he was with Rebel Bill Smith, they attempted to disrupt the presidential election in Lawrence County, Kentucky, by taking over the polls and forcing election officials to step aside while thirty of his men cast false ballots. Devil Anse's name was at the top of the list of men accused of tampering with the election. Although the prosecution failed to convict Hatfield, this indictment is evidence of his affiliation with Rebel Bill Smith during that era of the war.[260]

Oath of Allegiance taken by William Anderson "Devil Anse" Hatfield, May 4, 1865. National Archives.

Details of the famous feud itself are beyond the scope of this work; however, there were several legal actions against him later for incidents associated with the feud. Afterward, Devil Anse settled into a reasonably quiet and successful lifestyle. The 1880 U.S. Census identified him at age forty-one years as the owner of a large timber business, residing in Mingo County at Magnolia, West Virginia. He later experienced a dramatic conversion to Christianity on September 23, 1911, and was baptized by his friend and Confederate veteran, William "Uncle Dyke" Garrett near his home at Sarah Ann, West Virginia. Garrett is said to have quipped that he had "baptized the devil" and that it was his "proudest achievement." Devil Anse's friends and neighbors said he was "much changed" following his conversion and baptism. Ultimately, Devil Anse was mortal, and became ill with pneumonia, and died of a stroke on January 6, 1921. He is buried at the Hatfield Cemetery in Logan County.[261]

Summarily, Devil Anse remains one of the most mysterious and misrepresented characters in Appalachian lore, particularly the part of his life related to serving in the Confederate Army has often been inaccurately reported. Despite this, another veteran memorialized Hatfield in a 1900 article appearing in the Confederate Veteran Magazine as follows:

> Devil Anse always goes with a Winchester, a sack around his neck full of cartridges, a pair of good Smith and Wesson's, and I am told, that a good pair of Damascus blades luxuriate constantly from his boot legs. He was once a man of good property, and I was informed that the property he owned would bring now over fifty thousand dollars.
>
> He lives in a cabin about four miles from Logan, at the head of a creek, and his house is his castle. He virtually sleeps with one eye open, or as someone said, "sleeps on one eye at a time."
>
> He had been hounded by officers and enemies so long that he is ever alert and watchful; so much that, in addition to the five senses being all perfect, the boys say that he also has an eye in the back of his head. He is poor in worldly goods, when you hear that Devil Anse has been shot, it will not be in the back; he will have several piled around him. He was a good Confederate soldier and is far more to be pitied now in his near three-score and ten than condemned.[262]

Execution of McCoy Boys.
West Virginia State Archives.

Devil Anse Hatfield grave site. Sarah Ann, Logan County, West Virginia. The statue of Devil Anse is facing east, away from the state of Kentucky. This was done at his request according to Hatfield family tradition. Photo courtesy of WVATV Riding.

Close up of Devil Anse's grave marker. Photo by Heather New, Bloody Mingo Tours.

THE OTHER FEUD

Appendix

Appendix - Table 1
Hatfield Civil War Service

Name	Dates	Co.	Regiment	Rank	Misc.
Ephraim	9/61-3/63	B	1st VSL	Pvt	Age 54
Devil Anse	1861 3/62-4/62 4/63-12/63? 1/64?-5/65	Buchanan's Co. G B Partisan Co.	129th Va. Militia 2nd VSL 45th Bttn Smith's Bttn	? 1st Lt 1st Lt	Deserted
Ellison	7/62-4/63 5/63-10/63	I B	1st VSL 45th Bttn	Pvt 2nd Lt	Deserted
Floyd	9/61-11/61	Buchanan's Co.	129th Va. Militia	Pvt	
Valentine					
Andrew					
Larkin					
Ellison Mounts					
Jim Vance					

Notes: VSL is an abbreviation of Virginia State Line. Feud participants listed in order of familial relationship to Devil Anse: Elias, Ellison and Valentine were his brothers. Jim Vance was his maternal uncle. Ellison Mounts was a cousin; there has been some controversy over whether the Ephraim Hatfield found in VSL records was his father or a cousin; his father was born in 1811, and aged 51 years in 1861. Historian Otis K. Rice noted in his book, *The Hatfields & McCoys*, that Ephraim was his cousin based on G. Elliott Hatfield's 1974 genealogical study of the Hatfields. However, historian James Prichard argued that Ephraim was Devil Anse's father. Andrew and Larkin were his nephews, both sons of his sister Martha. All of Devil Anse's sons who later fought in the feud were born after 1861 and too young to have served in the Civil War. All men listed after Floyd Hatfield did not serve in the Civil War. There were no Hatfield feudists who served in the Union army, although several extended kinsmen were in Union regiments.

Appendix - Table 2
McCoy Civil War Service

Name	Dates	Co.	Regiment	Rank	Misc.
Randall	1863-65	- A	1st VSL? 10th KY Cav? 45th Battn?	Pvt	POW
James H.	12/61-5/65	D	5th KY Cav (US)	Pvt	
Asa Harmon	11/63-12/64	E	45th KY MI (US)	Pvt	Murdered
Samuel B.	1862-65	B	12th KY Cav (US)	Pvt	Age 12
Selkirk	12/62-4/63 5/63-11/63	A E	1st VSL 45th Bttn	2nd Sgt Pvt	AWOL
Andrew B.	9/1/63	E	45th Bttn	Pvt	Deserted
Uriah	12/62-3/63 5/63-?	A B	1st VSL 45th Bttn	2nd Cpl Pvt	
Hiram H.	12/61-7/65	K	3rd KY Cav (US)	Pvt	
William J.	5/63-3/64	E	45th Bttn	Pvt	
Wiley	10/62-3/63 1864	B	2nd Bttn Ky MI Rebel Bill Smith's Battalion	Pvt	Deserted
Wm. Thompson					
Floyd					
Jacob					
Asa Burris					

Notes: VSL is an abbreviation of Virginia State Line. Feudists' relationship to Randall McCoy: Asa H. and Samuel were his brothers. Asa Burris was a cousin; Asa Burris' son Lewis Jefferson (Jeff) McCoy has been cited as serving in both the 129th Va. Militia and 1st VSL but was aged two years in 1861. Other extended family members identified as feudists are Hiram H. McCoy, and his son William Johnson McCoy. The latter was Devil Anse's Brother-in-law. Six of fourteen McCoy feudists served in the Confederacy, and four were in Union regiments, while four feudists did not serve in the Civil War. Also, previous editions erroneously placed William Thompson in the 12th Kentucky Cavalry (US), but regimental muster rolls do not show his name. Randall McCoy's service is documented by Union prison records; his name does not appear on any of the unit muster rolls in which various writers claim he served. Andrew B. McCoy enlisted and deserted the same day. Note William Thompson was Randall's son-in-law; he should not be confused with William T. McCoy who served in Company D, 10th Kentucky Cavalry (Diamond's); this person was not a feudist (See CSR, RG 94, M319, Roll 53, National Archives).

Notes

Introduction

1. 1830, 1840, 1850 and 1860 United States Census and Slave Schedules. Record Group 29, Microfilm 19, 653, & 1358, pp. 91 (HW), (stamped) 289, Logan County, Va., June 1, 1860, Enumerated by B.S. Chapman. Washington, D.C.: National Archives and Records Administration; Dr. Coleman C. Hatfield and Robert Y. Spence. *The Tale of the Devil: The Biography of Devil Anse Hatfield.* (Charleston, WV: Quarrier Press, 2003), 17-26, 58. (Hereafter Coleman C. Hatfield)
2. Altina Waller. *Hatfields, McCoys and Social Change in Appalachia 1860-1900.* (Chapel Hill, NC: University of North Carolina Press, 1988), 2; Dean King. *The Hatfields and McCoys: The True Story*. (New York: Back Bay Books, 2013), 29; G. Elliot Hatfield, *The Hatfields,* Edited by Leonard Roberts and Henry P. Scalf. (Pikeville, KY: Big Sandy Historical Society, 1974, Revised 1988), 211; Ludwell H. Johnson (Ed.). "The Horrible Butcheries of West Virginia: Dan Cunningham

on the Hatfield-McCoy Feud: Ans' Hatfield War History." *West Virginia History,* Vol. 46, 1985-1986, 42. Dan Cunningham. "Murders in Jackson and Roane Counties, West Virginia." (1931) Manuscripts Collection, No. 364.152 C973, WV State Archives. Dan Cunningham was one of the detectives who sought to pin murder charges Devil Anse Hatfield during the feud era; he left a detailed account of Hatfield's Civil War service including many partisan guerrilla activities. However, many historians view his work as Union biased due to his father and brother being in the Union army, and negatively skewed toward the Hatfields because his brother was murdered by the Counts gang, known Hatfield supporters. See: James M. Prichard. "The Devil at Large: Anse Hatfield's War." in William C. Davis and James I. Robertson, Jr., *Virginia at War 1863.* (Lexington, KY: University of Kentucky Press, 2009), 78, n. 8.

3. Camp Chase Paroles, 1862-1865. Series 1543, Ohio Historical Society, Columbus Ohio; Records of Confederate Prisoners of War, 1861-1865, RG 109, M598, Randall McCoy, Roll 145, National Archives; Lisa Alther. *Blood Feud: The Hatfields and McCoys: The Epic Story of Murder and Vengeance.* (Guilford, Lyons Press, 2012), 35, 242, n. 43.
4. Otis K. Rice. *The Hatfields and McCoys.* (Lexington, Kentucky: University Press of Kentucky, 2010), 9; Waller, 2; 17-33; Prichard, 57.
5. Rice, 11; Coleman Hatfield, 65-69; Waller, 2; King, 26. There are other books which similarly cite inaccuracies in the feudists' Civil War service, discussed in later chapters.
6. John E. Pearce. *Days of Darkness: The Feuds of Eastern Kentucky.* (Lexington, KY: University of Kentucky Press, 1994), 1-8. This book covers several family conflicts in eastern Kentucky and the author generally acknowledges that many sources are from various family traditions; however, Pearce still makes a compelling case that the many such stories emerging in the war period and Reconstruction era are reflective of an enduring or unsettled sense of war-time tensions in the region.
7. R.E. Strange and D.E. Brown, Jr. "Home from the War: A Study of Psychiatric Problems in Vietnam Returnees." *American Journal of*

Psychiatry, Vol. 127(4), (Oct. 1970), 488-492; Hyer, L., Summers, M. N., Braswell, L., & Boyd, S. "Posttraumatic stress disorder: Silent problem among older combat veterans." *Psychotherapy: Theory, Research, Practice, Training, 32*(2), (1995), 348–364; David Behar. "Flashbacks and Posttraumatic Stress Symptoms among Combat Veterans." *Comprehensive Psychiatry*, Vol. 28(6), (Nov.-Dec. 1987), 459-466; T. Yager, R. Laufer, & M. Gallops. "Problems Associated with War Experience in Men of the Vietnam Generation." *Archive of General Psychiatry*, Vol. 41(4), (1984), 327-333; N.A. Sayer et al. "Reintegration Problems and Treatment Interests Among Iraq and Afghanistan Combat Veterans Receiving VA Medical Care." *Psychiatric Services*, Vol. 61(6), (June 2010), 589-597; C.W. Hoge, et. Al. "Combat Duty in Iraq and Afghanistan: Mental Health Problems and Barriers to Care." New England Journal of Medicine, Vol. 351(1), (July 1, 2004), 13-22. This brief list of studies is not intended as a comprehensive literature review, as there are hundreds of related studies published in the behavioral sciences. Further, the author is not suggesting that members of the Hatfield and McCoy feud had mental disorders per se but is rather intended to illustrate the common effects of combat service on veterans that doubtlessly had some effect on their social functioning.

8. G. Elliot Hatfield, 15-22, 183-200; Rice, 3-5.
9. Coleman C. Hatfield, 20-24; Waller, 35; Prichard, 35; G. Elliot Hatfield, x.
10. Ibid., Waller; Coleman Hatfield, 304; *Logan Telegraph* "Time-Dimmed Record of Early Logan County Families in 1852-1877 Period in Old Books Found at Pecks Mill." November 3, 1936. Newspapers on Microfilm, Logan Banner, Misc. Reels, M-6. WV State Archives. See also: Brandon R. Kirk Blog. Summary of Article posted online March 4, 2019: https://brandonraykirk.com/tag/joseph-hinchman/. Ulysses S. Hinchman later became a physician, pastor, and trader. The modern town of Man, West Virginia, is named after him.
11. Ancestry.com. *West Virginia, Deaths Index, 1853-1973* [database on-line]. Provo, UT, USA: Ancestry.com Operations, Inc., 2011, accessed

April 10, 2020. Levisa Levicy Chafin Hatfield's death certificate indicates she was married to Anse Hatfield April 18, 1861; *Ashland Daily Independent,* March 15, 1929 states Levisa Levicy Hatfield was Mrs. William Anderson Hatfield. Source: Ancestry.com. *Web: Boyd County, Kentucky, Ashland Daily Independent Obituary Index, 1922-1945, 1970-1973, 1998-2010* [database on-line]. Provo, UT, USA: Ancestry.com Operations, Inc., 2011. See also Coleman C. Hatfield, 58; King 25; G. Elliot Hatfield.

Chapter One

12. Lee A. Wallace. A Guide to Virginia Military Organizations 1861-1865. (Lynchburg, Virginia: H.E. Howard, 1986), 275; Records of the Colonial Militia through World War I. Ca. 1936, MS80-22, 50-53, WV State Archives.
13. Coleman C. Hatfield, 62-63, 304; Michael B. Graham. *The Coal River Valley in the Civil War*. (United Kingdom: History Press, 2014), 61-65; Department of Confederate Military Records, Accession No. 27684, 1861-1865. 129th Regiment Virginia Militia. 129th Regiment Virginia Militia, Series 2, Unit Records, Subseries 8, Militia, Box 36, Folder 15, Library of Virginia, Richmond, Virginia; Compiled Service Records, (CSR) 129th Regiment Virginia Militia, Record Group 109, Microfilm 324, Roll 1056; 187th Regiment Virginia Militia, Series 2, Unit Records, Subseries 8, Militia, Box 36, Folder 58-60, (See Oversized - Drawer 16), Library of Virginia, Richmond, Virginia; Linger, James C. *Confederate Military Organizations in West Virginia 1861-1865*. 8th Edition. (Tulsa OK: Privately published monograph, 2004), 20-21.
14. Prichard, 58.
15. Records of the Colonial Militia, WV State Archives; Virginia Code Chapter 23, Section 6, 1858. Cited in the *Journal of the Virginia House of Delegates, 1857-1858* (Richmond, VA: William F. Ritchie, Public Printer, 1857-1858), 392, 433, 557; see also: *Journal of the Senate of the Commonwealth of Virginia*, General Assembly. 1861. (Richmond, Virginia: J.E. Goode, Publisher), 152; *Journal of the Virginia House of Delegates, 1857-1858*, 392, 433, 557; WV AG Papers, Union Militia 1861-1865, AR-373, Box 21, Folder 1, Captain Edward Naret Letters, WV State Archives; *Star of Kanawha Valley* Newspaper, Buffalo, Va., May 21, 1860; OR, Series 1, Vol. 5, 501-503. Captain Edward Naret was the Adjutant of the 181st Regiment Virginia Militia in Putnam County during 1861-1862. Naret wrote several letters complaining to Governor Francis Pierpont because he was unable to fulfill recruiting quotas due to men fearing being sent far from their homes in the regular army, and for fear their families would

suffer retaliation from guerrillas and Southern citizens.

16. Yates Publishing. *U.S. and International Marriage Records, 1560-1900*, Virginia, [database on-line]. Provo, UT, USA: Ancestry.com Operations Inc, 2004. Devil Anse married Levicy Chafin on April 19, 1861 at Logan County, Virginia.
17. Coleman C. Hatfield, *62-69*; Waller, 2, 17, 32; King, 26, 33-34; Scott, 1-3; Wallace, 118-119; Otis K. Rice. *The Hatfields and McCoys.* (Lexington, Kentucky: University Press of Kentucky, 2010), 10-11; Virginia Infantry, Logan County Wildcats, Logbook, 1830-1900. Accession No. 1977/11.0206 (MS-59) Marshall University Special Collections (MUSC), Marshall University Library, Huntington, WV; James L. Scott. 36th Virginia Infantry. (Lynchburg, VA: H.E. Howard, 1987), 2-3; Department of Confederate Military Records, Accession No. 27684. 1861-1865. Series 2, Unit Records, Subseries 3, Infantry Units, 36th Virginia Infantry, Box 25, Folders 1-12, Library of Virginia; CSR, 36th Virginia Infantry, RG 94, M324, Roll 824, National Archives. The 36th Virginia Infantry was involved at the battles of Scary Creek and Carnifex Ferry in 1861 and were also at Fort Donelson in 1862. This regiment later saw heavy action in the Shenandoah Valley in 1864.
18. Coleman C. Hatfield, 304. Here, Coleman Hatfield did not refer to the company as the Logan Wildcats; however, this account is likely the basis of many writers referring to Devil Anse as "Captain Hatfield," although military records show he was never ranked higher than a 1st Lieutenant during the Civil War.
19. 1860 U.S. Census, No. 234, 37: www.fold3.com; *Logan Telegraph* "Time-Dimmed Record of Early Logan County Families in 1852-1877 Period in Old Books Found at Pecks Mill." November 3, 1936; See also: Brandon R. Kirk Blog, March 4, 2019: https://brandonraykirk.com/tag/joseph-hinchman/; *Logan Banner*, August 13, 1995; West Virginia Adjutant General Papers, Union Militia 1861-1865, AR-373, Box 12, Logan, Mason & Morgan Counties, Folder 1, Letter to Captain Joseph H. Hinchman from Lieutenant Colonel William H.H. Russell, 4th West Virginia Infantry, January 5, 1862. WV State Archives. Ulysses S. Hinchman was not only a

physician, but also later served as a pastor. The modern town of Man, West Virginia, is named after him using an abbreviation of the Hinchman name.

20. Ibid., *Logan Telegraph,* November 3, 1936; 1860 U.S. Census, Logan County, Ulysses S. Hinchman family, No. 234, 37; *Logan Banner*, August 13, 1995. Note also that both the *Logan Telegraph* and *Logan Banner* articles also mention a "12th Regiment" and could easily be misconstrued as the journal representing two separate militia organizations. However, the 12th Regiment Virginia Militia was in the 2nd Division, 3rd Brigade from Fluvanna County, Virginia. Hence that reference is erroneous. (cf. Wallace, 244-245).
21. Personal communications: (email and phone call) April 3, 2020. Mary Hinchman, Hinchman Historical Society, Lexington, Kentucky; Coleman C. Hatfield, 304. Unfortunately, at the time of this writing, the author was unable to locate the journal for the 129th Virginia Militia Regiment cited by Coleman Hatfield for personal review.
22. Wallace, 275; 129th Regiment Virginia Militia Records; CSR, 129th Regiment Virginia Militia.
23. Ibid; 129th Regiment Virginia Militia Records; CSR, 129th Regiment Virginia Militia.
24. Ibid.
25. Ibid.
26. Ibid.; CSR, 4th West Virginia Cavalry, RG 94, M508, Roll 41, National Archives; West Virginia Adjutant General Papers, Union Militia 1861-1865, AR-373, Box 12, Logan, Mason & Morgan Counties, Folder 2, Letter from Thomas Buchanan to Governor Arthur Boreman, July 14, 1865. WV State Archives.
27. 129th Regiment Virginia Militia Records, Library of Virginia; CSR, 129th Regiment Virginia Militia; Dr. R.A. Brock. *Virginia and Virginians, 1606-1888.* (Richmond, VA: H.H. Hardesty Publisher, 1888), 821-822; 1860 US Census, Logan County, Virginia, M653-1358, (see p. 289): www.rootsweb.com. John and Thomas Buchanan were originally from Tazewell County, Virginia. John was a farmer and in the timber business prior to the Civil War; he was elected

Sheriff of Logan County in 1868 and served until 1872. After the war, Thomas Buchanan served as Assessor for the State Auditor for two years and held the office of Logan County Clerk of Court, and later served as postmaster. Thomas also owned a great deal of land and extensive coal and timber interests.

28. Ira P. Hager. *Blue and Gray Battlefields*. Vol. 1. (Parsons, West Virginia, 1978), 27-30; 129th Regiment Virginia Militia Records, Library of Virginia; CSR, 129th Regiment Virginia Militia.
29. Hinchman Journal cited in *Logan Telegraph,* November 3, 1936 and reprinted in *Logan Banner*, August 13, 1995.
30. Ibid.
31. Ibid.
32. Ibid.
33. Coleman Hatfield, 63; 129th Regiment Virginia Militia Records; CSR, 129th Regiment Virginia Militia, Record Group 109, Microfilm 324, National Archives.
34. Hinchman Journal cited in *Logan Telegraph,* November 3, 1936 and reprinted in *Logan Banner*, August 13, 1995; Records of the Colonial Militia, WV State Archives; *Journal of the Senate of the Commonwealth of Virginia*, 1861, 152; Michael Egan. Edited by D.L. Philips. *The Flying Gray-Haired Yank or the Adventures of a Volunteer.* (Leesburg, VA: Gauley Press, 1992), 19-38; Wallace, iv-vii; *The Weekly Register*, March 6, 1862. Vol. 1(1), 4. Chronicling America Series, Library of Congress. Online: https://chroniclingamerica.loc.gov.
35. Ibid., Hinchman Journal; Terry Lowry. *22nd Virginia Infantry*. (Lynchburg, Virginia: H.E. Howard, 1988), 3. In 1861, the Kanawha Rifles mustered into the 22nd Virginia Infantry in Confederate service as Company H under Captain George Patton. Captain Patton was the great-grandfather of the famous World War II General Patton, and later became colonel of the regiment.
36. "Devil Anse Tells the True History of the Famous Hatfield-McCoy Feud." Wheeling Intelligencer newspaper. November 23, 1889. Vol. 38(78), 1. Chronicling America Series, Library of Congress. Online: https://chroniclingamerica.loc.gov. (hereafter Wheeling Intelligencer, November 23, 1889)

37. Ibid., *Wheeling Intelligencer*; 129th Regiment Virginia Militia Records; CSR, 129th Regiment Virginia Militia.
38. Ibid.; Department of Confederate Military Records, Accession No. 27684, 1861-1865. Series 2, Subseries 8, Militia, 187th Regiment Virginia Militia, Box 36, Folders 58-60, Library of Virginia; WV AG Papers, Union Militia, AR 373, Drawer 80, WV State Archives. Note that two companies of the 187th Regiment were Union, Company A and Captain C. Harless' Company; Prichard, 57, 78.
39. Ibid., *Wheeling Intelligencer*, Department of Confederate Military Records, Accession No. 27684, 1861-1865. Series 2, Unit Records, Subseries 3, Infantry Units, 45th Battalion Virginia Infantry, Militia, Box 30, Folder 66, Library of Virginia; CSR, 45th Battalion Virginia Infantry, RG 109, M861, Roll 70, National Archives.
40. Jack L. Dickinson. *Wayne County, West Virginia in the Civil War.* (Salem, Massachusetts: Higginson Book Company, 2003), 72-73; U.S. War Department, *The War of the Rebellion: A Compilation of the Official Records of the Union and Confederate Armies, 128 Vols.* (Washington, DC: Government Printing Office, 1881-1901), (hereafter OR), Series 1, Vol. 5, 1; *Ironton Register*, August 29, 1861; Robert Thompson. *Pioneers, Rebels and Wolves: A History of Wayne County.* (Wayne County, WV: Lulu.com, 2011), 102-103.
41. Ibid.; Frank Moore, (Ed.). *The Rebellion Record: A Diary of American Events, with Documents, Narratives, Illustrative Incidents, Poetry, Etc.* Vol. 3. (New York: G.P. Putnam, 1862), 14; Sandy Valley Advocate, Ca*tlettsburg (Ky.) Advocate*, August 28, 1861. University of Kentucky Archives.
42. *New York Times*, September 15, 1861.
43. *Ironton Register*, April 5, 1888; Dickinson, Wayne County WV in the Civil War, 72-73.
44. Moore, 14; *Ironton Register*, April 5, 1888.
45. *Ironton Register*, August 29, 1861; Dickinson, Wayne County WV in the Civil War, 72-73; Thompson, 102-103.
46. *New York Times*, September 15, 1861.
47. "Fights in Wayne Co., Va." *The Ironton Register*, August 29, 1861. LCCN: 84028882. Library of Congress.

48. Ibid.
49. *New York Times*, September 15, 1861; *Wayne County News*, July 4, 2018; Thompson, 103-104.
50. OR, Series 7, Supplement, Vol. 51, Part 1, 465, 468, 472; Boyd B. Stutler. *West Virginia in the Civil War*. (Charleston, WV: Education Foundation, Inc., 1966), 162-163; Jacob Dolson Cox. *Military Reminisces of the Civil War*, Vol.1. (Whitefish, MT: Kessinger Publishing, 2004 Reprint, Original 1900), 35; Michael B. Graham. *The Coal River Valley in the Civil War*. (United Kingdom: History Press, 2014), 49-53; "Details of the Boone Court House Fight." *Gallipolis Journal*, September 12, 1861. Online: Timeline of West Virginia: Civil War and Statehood, September 1, 1861. www.wvculture.org/history; OR, Series 1, Vol. 5, 2.
51. Ibid.
52. Ibid.; WV AG Papers, Union Militia Muster Rolls, Boone County, 187th Regiment, AR 373, Box 1, Folders 13, 15-18, Correspondence, (Peytona Home Guards), and Muster Rolls Drawer 80, WV State Archives. The Peytona Home Guards had members from Boone County as well as the Pond Fork area. There was also a small band of partisans from Logan and Wyoming Counties known as the Black Striped Company who were likely present at Boone Court House. Note also the two home guard companies are often misidentified as Companies B and I of the 8th West Virginia Volunteer Infantry at Boone Court House. While members of both units later mustered into those companies of the 8th West Virginia Infantry, the regiment did not formally organize until after the affair at Boone County Court House. Cf. CSR, (7th West Virginia Cavalry, formerly 8th West Virginia Volunteer Infantry) RG 94, M508, Rolls 77 & 82, National Archives.
53. "Late from the Kanawha: The Fight at Boone." *Gallipolis Journal*, September 12, 1861. Vol. 26(43), 4. Online: https://Chroniclingamerica.loc.gov; *Cleveland Morning Leader*, September 6, 1861. Vol. 15(211), 2. Online: https://Chroniclingamerica.loc.gov
54. Cox, Reminiscences, 35, OR Supplement Vol. 51, 465, 468, 472; Jeffrey A. Hill. The 26th Ohio Veteran Volunteer Infantry: The

Groundhog Regiment. (Bloomington, IN: Author House Publishing, 2010), 52; Graham, 56-57.
55. Graham, 54-55.
56. Ibid.; OR Supplement, Vol. 51, 465; Cox, Reminisces 35; *Gallipolis Journal*, September 12, 1861; "Fights in Wayne Co., Va." *The Ironton Register*, September 12, 1861.
57. Ibid., *Gallipolis Journal.* Note this newspaper indicated it was Companies B and D, 4th West Virginia, who led the initial advance and refused to fall back as ordered; General Cox's correspondence contradicts this information.
58. Ibid., Cox; *Gallipolis Journal*, September 12, 1861; Graham 60-61; *Ironton Register*, September 12, 1861.
59. OR, Series 1, Vol. 5, Part 1, 870; OR Supplement Vol. 51., 468, 472.
60. Ibid., OR Supplement Vol. 51; *Gallipolis Journal*, September 12, 1861; *Ironton Register*, September 12, 1861; OR, Vol. 5, Part 1, 870.
61. CSR, 129th Regiment Virginia Militia, Record of Events, RG 109, M324, Roll 1056, National Archives.
62. "Boone Court House, Va." *Richmond Daily Dispatch,* September 6, 1861; Vol. 20(55), Chronicling America, Library of Congress: www.chroniclingamerica.loc.gov.
63. *Gallipolis Journal*, September 12, 1861.
64. CSR, 129th Regiment Virginia Militia, Record of Events.
65. Ibid.
66. *Cincinnati Commercial.* October 3, 1861; *National Republican*, October 7, 1861.
67. *Chicago Daily Tribune*, October 9, 1861.
68. *Bucyrus Journal*, October 18, 1861.
69. *Cleveland Morning Leader*, September 12, 1861; *Evening Star* (Washington, DC), October 4, 1861; *National Republican,* October 7, 1861; *Chicago Daily Tribune*, October 9, 1861.
70. *Bucyrus Journal*, October 18, 1861; *Staunton Spectator*, September 25, 1861.
71. 129th Regiment Virginia Militia Records; CSR, 129th Regiment Virginia Militia.
72. Coleman C. Hatfield, 81; Terry Lowry. *The Battle of Scary Creek.*

(Charleston, WV: Quarrier Press, 1986), 23; 226; Richard Andre, Stan Cohen and Bill Wintz. *Bullets and Steel: The Fight for the Great Kanawha Valley 1861-1865.* (Charleston, West Virginia: Pictorial Histories Publishing, 1995), 55-57. Service records do not show Devil Anse was a member of the Sandy Rangers. Devil Anse was well known in his community prior to the Civil War and was friends with many veterans in not only Logan County, but also Cabell, Wayne and Boone Counties. Many of those men served in the 129th and 167th Regiments of Virginia Militia as well as the 36th Virginia Infantry, Virginia State Line and 45th Battalion Virginia Infantry. Post war reunions held by the United Confederate Veteran's Straton Camp of Logan County often showed Devil Anse, as well as men from those regiments in attendance; however, it was not required to have served exclusively in the 36th Virginia Infantry to attend meetings and reunions, so that is not reliable evidence Hatfield was part of the Logan Wildcats or Sandy Rangers. Camp Straton Reunion accounts are found in the *Logan Democrat* newspaper, September 19, 1912; October 26, 1911.

73. Ibid., Lowry.

74. Ibid.

75. Lowry; Jack L. Dickinson. *8th Virginia Cavalry.* (Lynchburg, VA: H.E. Howard, 1986), 13; Scott, 13; Department of Confederate Military Records 1859-1865, Series 2, Unit Records Subseries 3 Infantry, Accession No 27684, 36th Virginia Infantry, Box 25, Folder 4, "Lawson's Company" (Company D) Library of Virginia, Richmond, Virginia; Coleman C. Hatfield, 81-82; Prichard 67; Robert M. Thompson. *Twelve Pole Terror: The Legend of Rebel Bill Smith.* (Wayne, WV: R.M. Thompson Books, 2015), 47-48; Jeffrey C. Weaver. 45th Battalion Virginia Infantry, Smith and Count's Battalions Partisan Rangers. (Lynchburg, VA: H.E. Howard, 1994), 137, 148-149. The exact date the Sandy Rangers became part of the 8th Virginia Cavalry is unknown, but the author noted it was likely May 15, 1862. Interestingly, prior to mustering into the 8th Virginia Cavalry, this company was also attached to the 36th Virginia Infantry; that may also be the basis of various accounts claiming Devil Anse

was in the Logan Wildcats, who were Company D of that regiment. William S. "Rebel Bill" Smith was the antebellum neighbor of Colonel Milton J. Ferguson of Wayne County, who later commanded the 16th Virginia Cavalry and was also present at Scary Creek. Whether these relationships correlate to Devil Anse's presence there also, is unknown, but seems doubtful.

76. Waller, 2, 17; King, 33-34, 33-34, 354-355, n.2; Jones, 241; Rice, 11, 13-14; Coleman C. Hatfield, 62-68, 304; G. Elliott Hatfield. *The Hatfields.* Revised and edited by Leonard Roberts and Henry P. Scalf. (Paintsville, KY: Scaffold Press, 2012), 197; Coleman C. Hatfield, 62-68; Department of Confederate Military Records, 36th Virginia Infantry, Library of Virginia; CSR, RG 94, 36th Virginia Infantry, M324, Roll 824, National Archives.
77. Ibid., Waller; Jones, Rice, King.
78. Coleman C. Hatfield, 304; Logan Wildcats, Logbook, MUSC; *Logan Telegraph,* November 3, 1936; *Logan Banner*, August 13, 1995.
79. Coleman C. Hatfield; *Kanawha Valley Star*, newspaper, May 11, 1861. Newspapers on Microfilm, Misc. Reels, Misc. Reels M-126. WV State Archives.
80. Ibid.
81. *Wheeling Intelligencer*, November 23, 1889; Records of the 36th Virginia Infantry, Library of Virginia; CSR, 36th Virginia Infantry.
82. Coleman C. Hatfield, 63.
83. Ibid., 63-64.
84. Ibid., 82-83; Prichard, 60; King, 25, 27.

Chapter Two

85. Department of Confederate Military Records, 1861-1865. Accession No. 27684, Series 2, Unit Records, Subseries 7, Virginia State Line, Box 34, Folder 1, Library of Virginia, Richmond, Virginia; CSR, Virginia State Line, RG 94, M324, Roll 1066, National Archives.
86. Randall Osborne and Jeffrey C. Weaver, *The Virginia State Rangers and Virginia State Line, (Lynchburg, VA: H.E. Howard, 1994)*, 23-24.
87. Ibid., 24-25.
88. Hatfield, C., 61.
89. *West Virginia, Births Index, 1804-1938* [database on-line]. Provo, UT, USA: Ancestry.com Operations, Inc., 2011. WV State Archives; J.L. Scott. *36th Virginia Infantry, 10-15.*
90. Prichard, 56-61.
91. Ibid., 60-61; Pike County Kentucky Tax Assessment Book (1861), and Pike County Civil Cases No.'s 2377 and 2373, Kentucky Department of Libraries and Archives (KYDA). Cited in Prichard, 60.
92. West Virginia Adjutant Generals Papers, (WV AG) Union Militia, 1861-1865, AR373, Box 28, Captain Uriah Runyon's Company Roll, WV State Archives; WV AG Papers, Pierpont-Samuels Collection, AR1722, Letter of September 21, 1862 from William Ratcliff et al. to Pierpont requesting arms for three new companies of the 167th Regiment Virginia Militia, WV State Archives.
93. Prichard, 60.
94. Osborne and Weaver, *The Virginia State Rangers and Virginia State Line*, 27-28.
95. Ibid., 201; Virginia State Line Records.
96. Ibid., 42; Joseph Geiger, Jr. *Civil War in Cabell County 1861-1865.* (Charleston, West Virginia, Pictorial Histories Publishing, 1991), 23-36.
97. Ibid., Osborne and Weaver, 50. August 23, 1862 Letter from Hounshell, D.S. and Halsey, S.P cited in text.
98. Ibid.

99. Ibid., 72-76.
100. Ibid., 77-78; *Lynchburg Virginian*, October 24, 1862; Jasper E. Sutherland. *Pioneer Recollections of Southern West Virginia. (Clintwood, West Virginia: Mullins Printing*, originally published October 1862, reprinted 1984) cited in R. Osborne & Jeffrey C. Weaver, 78.
101. Ibid.
102. Ibid.
103. Ibid., 80.
104. Ibid., 82.
105. Ibid.
106. Ibid., 57-59; Preston, John D. *The Civil War in the Big Sandy Valley.* (Baltimore, Maryland: Gateway Press, 2008, Second Ed.), 140-142. (Hereafter Preston)
107. Ibid., 85-90.
108. Ibid.
109. Ibid.
110. Prichard, 62-63; CSR, 45th Kentucky Mounted Infantry, RG 94, M397, Roll 437; Medical Descriptive List, U.S. Army General Hospital, Lexington, Kentucky, Vol. 13(1), 1, Kentucky Department of Libraries and Archives, Frankfort, Kentucky; Letters of April 7, 1863 signed by Dr. William P. Morgan, U.S. Army Surgeon to the Army Surgeon General at Annapolis, Maryland, and A. Paulin: in Asa Harmon McCoy's Personal Documents, CSR, RG 94, M397, Roll 506, National Archives; Hewett, J.B. *Roster of Union Soldiers, 1861-1865.* 2000. Vol. 18, Kentucky & Tennessee. Wilmington, NC: Broadfoot Publishing, p. 226.
111. Ibid., Prichard, 62-63; it is doubtful the slave "Mose" met the following criteria, but if this account is factual, he would likely have obtained the money from one of the Clines: *The Code of Virginia. Second Edition. Including Legislation to the Year 1860* (Richmond: Ritchie, Dunnavant & Co., 1860), No. 12, 508-510. Slaves were subject to harsh physical punishment because the could not pay fines, i.e. having no money. Section 12 also notes "Any person who shall permit an insane, aged, or infirm slave owned by him or under his control, to go at large without adequate provision for his support, shall

be punished by fine not exceeding fifty dollars, and the overseers of the poor of the county or corporation, in which such slave may be found, shall provide for his maintenance…" Since he was said to have been capable of fighting, it is unlikely that Pete met the latter criteria to obtain money.

112. Ibid.
113. Ibid.
114. Micajah Woods Papers, Letter to his father, December 1862. Robert Osborne and Jeffrey C. Weaver cite Wood's letters extensively in their excellent book, *The Virginia State Rangers and Virginia State Line.* Micajah Woods, was born on May 17, 1844 in Albemarle County, Virginia. The eldest son of a family of ten children, he received his early education at Lewisburg Academy, the military school at Charlottesville, and the Bloomfield Academy. In August 1861, at the age of seventeen, he joined the Confederate Army as aide-de-camp on the staff of General John B. Floyd in West Virginia. He spent the winter of 1861-1862 at the University of Virginia, being under military age. In May 1862, Woods joined the Second Virginia Cavalry (Co. K) and fought under "Stonewall" Jackson at Port Republic, under J. E. B. Stuart in the Northern Virginia raids, and in the battles of Second Manassas, Crampton's Gap, and Sharpsburg.
115. Ibid.
116. Osborne and Weaver, 77-78.
117. Micajah Woods papers: cited in Osborne and Weaver, 81.
118. Ibid., Osborne and Weaver, 81.
119. Ibid., 68-69, 73-78, 97-99.
120. Ibid., 115.
121. Micajah Woods papers: cited in Prichard, 64.
122. Osborne and Weaver, 114-121.
123. Ibid.
124. Ibid., 109-110; 112, 114, 116-119.
125. Ibid., 110, 114-119.

Chapter Three

126. Waller, 17-33; Department of Confederate Military Records, Accession No. 27684, Series 2, Unit Records, Subseries 3: 45th Battalion Virginia Infantry Records, Box 30, Folder 66, (Buchanan's Company), Library of Virginia, Richmond, Virginia; CSR, 45th Battalion Virginia Infantry, RG 94, M397, Roll 437, National Archives; Jeffrey C. Weaver. *45th Battalion Virginia Infantry, Smith & Count's Battalions of Partisan Rangers*. (Lynchburg, Virginia: H.E. Howard, 1994), 21.
127. Ibid., Weaver, 10-15; Elliot G. Hatfield. *The Hatfields*. Revised and edited by Leonard Roberts and Henry P. Scalf. (Pikeville, Kentucky: The Big Sandy Valley Historical Society, 1988), 197; Waller, 31.
128. Ibid., Weaver, 20-25; "United States Census, 1860." Database with images. *Family Search*. http://FamilySearch.org: 21 March 2020. From "1860 U.S. Federal Census - Population." Database. *Fold3.com*. http://www.fold3.com. Citing NARA microfilm publication M653. Washington, D.C.: National Archives and Records Administration, n.d.
129. Ibid.
130. Weaver, 20-25; CSR, 45th Battalion Virginia Infantry.
131. Ibid., Weaver, 28, 32.
132. Ibid., 32; OR, Series 1, Vol. 23, Part 1, 5; 818-820; Weaver, 30-34; Report of the Adjutant General of the State of Kentucky. Vol. 2 1861-1866. (Frankfurt, Kentucky: John H. Harney, Public Printer, 1867), 425. The latter states that Colonel John Dil's regiment, 39th Kentucky Infantry, fought at Pond Creek near Pikeville in June 1863.
133. Ibid, Weaver, 32-33.
134. Ibid.; OR, Series 1, Vol. 23, Part 1, 5, 818-820. Historic sources conflict as to which side of the Tug River the battle of Pond Creek was fought upon. The majority appear to suggest it was in Pike County, Kentucky.
135. "A Fight in Western Virginia." *Lynchburg Virginian* July 18, 1863; Weaver, 33.
136. OR, Series 1, Vol. 23, Part 1, 5; 818-820; Weaver, 32-34; Osborne

and Weaver, 85-86; CSR, 45th Battalion Virginia Infantry; Camp Chase Paroles, 1862-1865. Series 1543, Ohio Historical Society, Columbus Ohio; Records of Confederate Prisoners of War, 1861-1865, RG 109, M598, Roll 145, National Archives; Muster Rolls of Paroled and Exchanged Confederate Prisoners of War, 1861-1865, RG 109, PI101, Id. No. 652414, National Archives; CSR, Miscellaneous Papers and Slips Belonging in Confederate Records. RG 109, M347, Roll 351, (Cat. No. 2133276), National Archives. Note the fold3.com site for the latter does not contain records for Randall McCoy in Miscellaneous Kentucky documents: CSR, RG 109, M319, Roll 136, National Archives; Rice, 11; Prichard, 57; King, 35, 355, n. 7; Tom E. Dotson. *The Hatfield & McCoy Feud After Kevin Costner: Rescuing History*. (North Charleston, South Carolina, Createspace.com, 2014) 110. Much thanks to retired United States Air Force Master Sergeant Edward McCoy, a descendent of Randall McCoy, for sharing information related to the McCoy patriarch's imprisonment.

137. Ibid.; Rice 10-11; Prichard, 57; King, 35-26, 355, n. 7; Alther, 242, n. 43. Lisa Alther cited page 72 in the Second Edition of *The Other Feud* as the source for her claim that Randall McCoy had no military service. However, that edition made the same assertion, as in 2011 when it was printed, the author was not aware of prison records or service records indicating McCoy was imprisoned at Camp Chase and Camp Douglas.

138. Ibid.; King, 35, 355, n. 7; Dotson, 110; 45th Battalion Virginia Infantry and Virginia State Line Records, Library of Virginia; CSR 45th Battalion Virginia Infantry; CSR Virginia State Line; CSR 10th Kentucky Cavalry, RG 94, M319, Roll 55, National Archives; 1860 U.S. Census; https://www.geni.com/people/Randolph-Randall-McCoy: see notes by Maria Edmonds-Zediker, Volunteer Curator, June 16, 2019; Ancestry.com. *Kentucky, County Marriage Records, 1783-1965* [database on-line]. Lehi, UT, USA: Ancestry.com Operations, Inc., 2016.

139. CSR, RG 94, 10th Kentucky Cavalry, M319, Roll 53 (Diamond's); CSR, 10th Kentucky Mounted Infantry, RG 94, M319, Roll 55; CSR,

10th Kentucky Cavalry (Johnson's) RG 94, M319, Roll 55; Prichard 63; King, 77. King cites a 2012 interview with a Chafin family descendent; while intriguing, such information is should be viewed with caution.

140. Records of Confederate Prisoners of War, National Archives; Muster Rolls of Paroled and Exchanged Confederate Prisoners of War, National Archives; Virginia State Line Records, Library of Virginia; CSR 45th Battalion Virginia Infantry; CSR Virginia State Line; CSR, RG 94, 10th Kentucky Cavalry (Diamond's), RG 94, M319, Roll 53, National Archives; CSR, 10th Kentucky Mounted Infantry, RG 94, M319, Roll 55, National Archives; CSR, 10th Kentucky Cavalry (Johnson's) RG 94, M319, Roll 55, National Archives.
141. Ibid., CSR, 10th Kentucky Cavalry; CSR, 10th Kentucky Mounted Infantry; CSR, 10th Kentucky Cavalry (Johnson's); CSR, 13th Kentucky Cavalry, RG 94, M319, Roll 67, National Archives; John Britton Wells & James M. Prichard. *10th Kentucky Cavalry, CSA: May's, Trimble's, Diamond's "Yankee Chasers."* (Baltimore, Maryland: Gateway Press, 1996), 3-14; 22-24. (Hereafter Wells & Prichard)
142. Coleman C. Hatfield, 61-79; Waller, 17.
143. *Floyd County Times* May 18, 1988.
144. 1860 US Census, Logan County, Virginia, M653-1358, (Page 289): www.rootsweb.com; Ulysses Hinchman Journal for the 129th Regiment Virginia Militia; 129th Regiment Virginia Militia Records, Library of Virginia; CSR, 129th Regiment Virginia Militia; WV AG Papers, Union Militia, AR-373, Box 12, WV State Archives.
145. Weaver, 108; King, 77. King cites a 2012 interview with a Chafin family descendent; while intriguing, such information is should be viewed with caution; *Logan Banner*, December 2, 1938. Newspapers on Microfilm, Misc. Rolls, WV State Archives; Prichard, 65-66; Weaver, 165-169.
146. Ibid., *Logan Banner*.
147. Prichard, 64; Dan Cunningham, "Murders in Jackson and Roane Counties, West Virginia." (1931); Johnson, 42; cited in Prichard, 64:

Pike County Kentucky Circuit Court Cases No. 2155, 2177, 2355, 2386, and 2774.

148. Ibid. Cited in Prichard, 64: Pike County Kentucky Circuit Court Cases No. 2155, 2177, 2355, 2386, and 2774.

149. F.S. Harris. "Noted Character of West Virginia." *Confederate Veteran,* October 1900, 205-206.

150. Prichard, 64.

151. 45th Battalion Virginia Infantry Records; CSR, 45th Battalion Virginia Infantry; *The Lynchburg Virginian.* July 18, 1863, cited in Weaver, 33.

152. Prichard, 64.

153. Ibid.; OR, Series 1, Vol. 23, Part 1, 5; 818-820.

154. *The Lynchburg Virginian.* July 18, 1863, cited in Weaver, 33.

155. 45th Battalion Virginia Infantry Records; CSR, 45th Battalion Virginia Infantry; OR, Series 1, Vol. 23, Part 1, 5; 818-820.

156. Weaver, 24

157. Truda Williams McCoy. *The McCoys: Their Story as told to the Author by Eyewitnesses and Descendants.* (Pikeville, Kentucky: Preservation Council Press of Pike County, 2000), 74, 225; Waller, 36.

158. Ibid.

159. Stephen W. Snuff. *The Blood Feud: Devil Anse Hatfield and The Real McCoys.* (British Columbia: Trufford Publishing, 2012), 35; 45th Battalion Virginia Infantry Records; CSR, 45th Battalion Virginia Infantry.

160. Ibid., CSR; Waller, xii, *Hatfield Abbreviated Genealogy*, xii.

161. Weaver, 34-38.

162. CSR, 45th Battalion Virginia Infantry. The supply receipts Devil Anse signed are in his service file.

163. Weaver, 38.

164. Ibid. 45th Battalion Virginia Infantry Records; 45th Battalion Virginia Infantry.

165. Ibid.

166. Ibid.

167. *Wheeling Intelligencer* newspaper. November 23, 1889.

168. Ibid., 39-41; OR, Series 1, Vol. 29, Part 1, 493-494.

169. Ibid.
170. Ibid.
171. Ibid., 41-42.
172. Ibid., 42.
173. Ibid.; OR Series 1, Vol. 29, Part 2, 556.
174. Ibid., Weaver, 42.
175. Weaver, 43-44; *Gallipolis Journal,* February 18, 1864; OR, Supplement, Vol. 2, 73, 806; OR Series 1, Vol. 51, Part 1, 211; OR Series 1, Vo. 33, 112; *Ironton Register,* February 4, 1864.
176. Ibid., Dickinson. *Wayne County in the Civil War,* 97-100.
177. Weaver, 43.
178. Coleman C. Hatfield, 78-81.
179. Ibid.,79-80; Records of the Adjutant and Inspector General's Department. Records relating to courts-martial, 1861-65, RG 109, M836, National Archives. There is no record of Devil Anse undergoing a Court Martial or Court of Inquiry found in records from the 45th Battalion Virginia Infantry as Hatfield family tradition claims as related to his desertion.
180. Ibid., 80-81.
181. Rice, 10-11.
182. Ibid., 11.
183. Waller, 31-32.
184. Ibid., 11; 45th Battalion Virginia Infantry Records; CSR, 45th Battalion Virginia Infantry, Prichard, 67.

Chapter Four

185. *Wheeling Intelligencer*, November 23, 1889.
186. Weaver, 138-139.
187. Weaver, 137-138; King, 11-12, 33; Rice, 11-12; Prichard, 67-68; Coleman C. Hatfield, 81; *Wheeling Intelligencer,* November 23, 1889. Prichard cited two letters written by William S. "Rebel Bill" Smith of August 16, 1864 and October 12, 1889; In the former, Hatfield was not listed among Smith's company commanders in the letter to Confederate Adjutant and Inspector General Samuel Cooper; however, in the latter, he wrote to Kentucky Governor Simon B. Buckner, offering to bring Devil Anse and other Hatfield's to justice during the feud era. In the same document he reported Hatfield had led a company in his partisan battalion during 1864-1865. Cited in Prichard, 68, 82 n. 66 & 68. See: Records of the Adjutant and Inspector General's Department, Letters and Telegrams Sent & Received, 1861-1865. RG 109, M410, National Archives. (August 16, 1864 Letter); See also: Public Records Division, Governor Simon B. Buckner Papers, Records pertaining to Applications for Requisitions (Returning Fugitives to Kentucky), Identifier No. 04538-RG1189, KDLA.
188. Virgil Carrington Jones. *The Hatfields and the McCoys.* (Chapel Hill, NC: University of North Carolina Press, 1948, First Ed.), 14.
189. Ibid.
190. Ibid., 15-16.
191. Ibid., 16. Devil Anse never obtained rank higher than 1st Lieutenant during the Civil War, and was in Company B, 45th Battalion Virginia Infantry according to his service files. While there is evidence that he served in the militia, Jones omitted his service in the Virginia State Line.
192. Ibid., 16.
193. G. Elliott Hatfield, 163-169; Tom E. Dotson. *The Hatfield & McCoy Feud After Kevin Costner: Rescuing History*. (North Charleston, SC: Createspace.com, 2014), 108.
194. Prichard, 67; Waller, 2, 31-33, Rice, 11-14; King, 33; Coleman C.

Hatfield, 81-82.
195. Coleman C. Hatfield, 81.
196. Weaver, 137.
197. Waller, 31.
198. Weaver, 137-138; Prichard, 67.
199. Dickinson, *8th Virginia Cavalry*, 13-14; Coleman C. Hatfield, 81; Thompson, 42-48; CSR, RG 94, M324, Roll 85, National Archives; Department of Confederate Military Records, 1859-1865, Accession No. 27684, Series 2, Unit Records, Subseries 2, Cavalry Regiments, 8th Virginia Cavalry, Box 15, Folder 44, n.d. Library of Virginia, Richmond, VA.
200. Ibid.; CSR, RG 94, M319, Roll 21, National Archives; Weaver, 137-138.
201. Ibid., Weaver, 138.
202. Prichard, 67; Weaver, 148-151.
203. *Ironton Register*, March 30, 1864; Weaver, 143-144.
204. Ibid., Weaver, 145; CSR 45th Battalion Virginia Infantry Records. Records show a Private James Henry Cook, Company C, 45th Battalion Virginia Infantry enlisted on May 18, 1862, at Wyoming County and deserted on September 1, 1863; however, we cannot be certain this is the same Henry Cook in the anecdote.
205. Ibid., 145-146.
206. Ibid., 145.
207. Ibid.
208. Prichard, 68; CSR, 39th Kentucky Infantry, RG 94, M397, Roll 429, National Archives; Pike County Kentucky Circuit Court Case No. 2074; Lawrence County Kentucky Circuit Court Civil Case No. 3183; Commonwealth vs. Melvin Lawson, et al., Box 13, Lawrence County Circuit Court Criminal Indictments, KDLA; Cited in Prichard, 82, n. 69, 72.
209. Ibid. Ellison Hatfield's name appeared as "Allison" Hatfield in court records, but there was no one by that name in Devil Anse's immediate family.
210. Ibid., Prichard, 69-70; Johnson, "Horrible Butcheries of West Virginia", 40. Asbury Hurley was also related to the Cline family by

marriage.
211. Weaver, 151.
212. Ibid.
213. Arthur I. Boreman Papers, Letter of August 31, 1864 and report of capture March 20, 1865 by Captain B.R. Haley; Weaver, 151-153.
214. Ibid., Arthur I. Boreman Papers, Letter from C. B. Webb, October 12, 1864.
215. Prichard, 71; Weaver, 152, 159; Scott C. Cole. *34th Battalion Virginia Cavalry*. (Lynchburg, KY: H.E. Howard, 1993), 9532.
216. *Weekly Register*, Vol. 3(30), November 3, 1864. Library of Congress.
217. Ibid.
218. *Louisville Daily Journal*, November 12, 1864, Vol. 33(2), Library of Congress; Weaver 160.
219. Ibid., November 22, 1864; Lawrence County, Kentucky Circuit Court Order Book, Vol. 6, 449: cited in Prichard, 71, 83, n. 87, 88.
220. Sutherland, *Pioneer Recollections,* cited in Weaver, 161; Arthur I. Boreman Papers, Letter from C. B. Webb, October 12, 1864.
221. Ibid.
222. Weaver, 164-165; OR, Series 1, Vol. 43, Part 2, 737-738.
223. Ibid., West Virginia, Births Index, WV State Archives.
224. CSR, 45th Battalion Virginia Infantry Records. Devil Anse's Oath of Allegiance is found in the CSR material; Weaver, 169-170.

Chapter Five

225. 1860 US Census & Slave Schedules; Prichard, 72-73; Waller, 2, 18, 30; Jones, 51-53; Rice, 13-14; Coleman C. Hatfield, 84-86.
226. West Virginia AG Papers, AR373, Box 28, Captain Uriah Runyon's Company Roll, WV State Archives; Pierpont-Samuels Collection, AR1722, Letter of September 21, 1862 from William Ratcliff et al. to Pierpont requesting arms for three new companies of the 167th Regiment Virginia Militia, WV State Archives; Letter of April 7, 1863 signed by Dr. William P. Morgan, U.S. Army Surgeon to the Army Surgeon General at Annapolis, Maryland, and A. Paulin: in Asa Harmon McCoy's Personal Documents, CSR, RG 94, M397, Roll 506, National Archives; Coleman C. Hatfield, 64; Rice, 36-39; King, 24-30.
227. Ibid.; Osborne and Weaver, 85-89.
228. Letter of April 7, 1863 signed by Dr. William P. Morgan, U.S. Army Surgeon to the Army Surgeon General at Annapolis, Maryland, and A. Paulin: in Asa Harmon McCoy's Personal Documents, CSR, RG 94, M397, Roll 506, National Archives; CSR, 5th Kentucky Infantry, RG 94, M397, 198, National Archives; Report of the Adjutant General of the State of Kentucky. Vol. 1, 1861-1866. (Frankfort, KY: J. Harney, Printer, 1866), 684-716. Note that CSR can be prone to transcription errors, although Asa Harmon McCoy's name is not found in those documents.
229. CSR, Asa Harmon McCoy's Personal Documents; CSR, 45th Kentucky Mounted Infantry, RG 94, M397, Roll 437; Report of the Adjutant General of the State of Kentucky, Vol. 2, 458-459; see also Hewett, J.B. Roster of Union Soldiers, 1861-1865. 2000. Vol. 18, Kentucky & Tennessee. Wilmington, NC: Broadfoot Publishing, 226; Prichard 72.
230. Ibid., CSR, 45th Kentucky Mounted Infantry; Report of the Adjutant General of the State of Kentucky, Vol. 2; Prichard, 72-73; Coleman C. Hatfield, 84-86; Waller, 17-18; Rice, 13-14, Jones, 16; King, 36-37; William Ely. *The Big Sandy Valley: A History of the People and Country from the Earliest Settlement to the Present Time.*

(Cattlettsburg, KY: Central Methodist, 1887), 203-204. Cited in King, 36-37.

231. Coleman C. Hatfield, 63-64.

232. Ibid.

233. Prichard, 65.

234. Ibid., 64; Johnson, 42; Pike County Circuit Court Cases 2155, 2177, 2386, and 2774, KDLA. Cited in Prichard, 81, n. 51.

235. Virginia State Line Records, Library of Virginia, Richmond, Virginia; CSR, Virginia State Line, RG 94, M324, Roll 1066, National Archives; Osborne and Weaver, 50, 72-78; Prichard, 60-63.

236. "Devil Anse Tells How." *Bluefield Daily Telegraph,* October 22, 1920. Newspapers on Microfilm, Misc. Rolls, WV State Archives; This article is also found at: Call No. NP 7002, Control No. SN86092605, Library of Congress; Prichard, 75.

237. Waller, 17; Prichard 74-75; Pike County Circuit Court Cases 2774 and 2589, KDLA; see also CSR, 39th Kentucky Mounted Infantry, and 1890 U.S. Veterans Census, Pike County, KDLA: Cited in Prichard 84, n. 102, 103. See also Hatfield and McCoy Genealogical tables in Waller, xiv-xvii; and Rice, appendix and Table 2 herein.

238. Ibid. Prichard, 76; McCoy, 11.

239. Waller, 17.

240. Prichard 73-74; Rice, 4; King 38; Yates Publishing. *U.S. and International Marriage Records, 1560-1900* [database on-line]. Provo, UT, USA: Ancestry.com Operations Inc, 2004. *Kentucky and West Virginia, Births Indexes, 1804-1938* [database on-line]. Provo, UT, USA: Ancestry.com Operations, Inc., 2011; See also Hatfield and McCoy Genealogical tables in Waller, xiv-xvii and Rice, Appendix and Tables 1 & 2 herein.

241. Seth A. Nichols. "Let Us Bury and Forget: Civil War Memory and Identity in Cabell County, West Virginia, 1865-1915." 2016. Unpublished Thesis, Marshall University Department of History, 1-12; 14-22; 27-39; Theses, Dissertations and Capstones. 1066. http://mds.marshall.edu/etd/1066.

Chapter Six

242. Rice, 14-15; Waller, 2, 17-18; Prichard 57; King, 31-33; Preston, 244.
243. Nichols, vii, 1-17, 14-22.
244. Ibid.; Prichard, 75.
245. Ibid.; Prichard, 76-77; Nichols, 32-34.
246. Waller, 17-18; 194.
247. Nichols, 32-33.
248. Weaver, 171.
249. Ibid.
250. Preston, 250.
251. Ibid.; Wells and Prichard, 95.
252. Strange and Brown, Jr. 488-492; Hyer, L., et al., 348–364; Behar, 459-466; Yager, et al., 327-333; Sayer et al., 589-597; Hoge, et. Al., 13-22. As noted in the Introduction, this brief list of studies is not a comprehensive literature review, nor does the author suggest that members of the Hatfield and McCoy feud had any specific mental disorders per se, but these data are cited to contextually illustrate the common effects of combat service on veterans.
253. Ibid.
254. Waller, 17-18; Rice 10-13; Prichard, 57.
255. 45th Battalion Records, Library of Virginia; CSR, 45th Battalion Virginia Infantry; CSR, Virginia State Line Records; Weaver, 186.
256. CSR, Union Regiments, 5th Kentucky Cavalry, RG 94, M397, Roll 55 (James H.); 45th Kentucky Mounted Infantry, RG 94, M397, Roll 437 (Asa Harmon); 12th Kentucky Cavalry, RG 94, M397, Roll 119 (Samuel B.); 3rd Kentucky Cavalry, RG 94, M397, Roll 32 (Hiram), National Archives.
257. Ibid., CSR, Hiram McCoy; Department of Confederate Military Records, Accession No. 27684, Series 2, Unit Records, Subseries 3: 45th Battalion Virginia Infantry Records, Box 30, Folder 66, (Buchanan's Company), (Thomas McCoy) Library of Virginia, Richmond, Virginia; CSR, 45th Battalion Virginia Infantry, RG 94, M397, Roll 437, (Devil Anse) National Archives; See also Osborne

and Weaver, 226. CSR, 2nd Battalion Mounted Infantry, RG 94, M319, Roll 21, (Wiley McCoy) National Archives); See also Weaver, 186. Note previous editions of this book erroneously listed Wiley McCoy as serving in the 45th Kentucky Mounted Infantry (US); however, while there was a Wyley McCoy who enlisted in Co. B, 45th Kentucky Mounted Infantry at Catlettsburg, KY, on September 6, 1863, from Russell County, VA, he died of bronchitis in the Union Army hospital at Ashland, KY, on November 5, 1863. Hence, Wyley McCoy could not have been a feudist. (cf. CSR, RG 94, 45th Kentucky Mounted Infantry (US), M397, Roll 497, National Archives.)

258. *Wheeling Intelligencer*, November 23, 1889.

Chapter Seven

259. Pike County Circuit Court Case 2074; Lawrence County Circuit Court Civil Case 3183.
260. Lawrence County Circuit Court Order Book No. 6:449. Cited in Prichard 68.
261. Coleman C. Hatfield, 256-258; Waller, 237-238, 206-234; Rice, 121; 1880 United States Census. Database with images. *Family Search*. FamilySearch.org: 2 April 2020. Citing NARA microfilm publication RG 29, M19. Washington, D.C.
262. Harris, 205-206.

Bibliography

Books

Alther, Lisa. Blood Feud: The Hatfields and McCoys: The Epic Story of Murder and Vengeance. (Guilford, Lyons Press, 2012).

Andre, Richard, Stan Cohen and Bill Wintz. *Bullets and Steel: The Fight for the Great Kanawha Valley 1861-1865.* (Charleston, West Virginia: Pictorial Histories Publishing, 1995).

Dr. R.A. Brock. *Virginia and Virginians, 1606-1888.* (Richmond, VA: H.H. Hardesty Publisher, 1888).

Britton, John Wells & James M. Prichard. *10th Kentucky Cavalry, C.S.A.: May's, Trimble's, Diamond's "Yankee Chasers."* (Baltimore, Maryland: Gateway Press, 1996), Chapter One.

Cole, Scott C. 34th Battalion Virginia Cavalry. (Lynchburg, VA: H.E. Howard, 1993).

Cox, Jacob Dolson. *Military Reminisces of the Civil War*, Vol.1. (Whitefish, MT: Kessinger Publishing, 2004 Reprint, Original 1900).

Crawford, T.C. *An American Vendetta*. (United Kingdom: Woodland Press, 2013; original published 1889).

Dickinson, Jack L. *Wayne County, West Virginia in the Civil War.* (Salem, Massachusetts: Higginson Book Company, 2003).

_____, 16th Virginia Cavalry. (Lynchburg, VA: H.E. Howard, 1989).

_____, 8th Virginia Cavalry (Lynchburg, VA: H.E. Howard, 1986).

Dotson, Tom E. *The Hatfield and McCoy Feud After Kevin Costner: Rescuing History.* (North Charleston, South Carolina, Createspace.com, 2014).

Egan, Michael. D.L. Philips. (Ed.). *The Flying Gray-Haired Yank or the Adventures of a Volunteer.* (Leesburg, VA: Gauley Press, 1992).

Ely, William. *The Big Sandy Valley: A History of the People and Country from the Earliest Settlement to the Present Time.* (Cattlettsburg, KY: Central Methodist, 1887).

Geiger, Joseph Jr. *Civil War in Cabell County 1861-1865.* (Charleston, West Virginia, Pictorial Histories Publishing, 1991).

Graham, Michael B. *The Coal River Valley in the Civil War.* (United States: History Press, 2014).

Hager, I.P. *Blue and Gray Battlefields.* Vol. 1. (Parsons, West Virginia, 1978).

Hatfield, Dr. Coleman C and Robert Y. Spence. *The Tale of the Devil: The Biography of Devil Anse Hatfield.* (Charleston, West Virginia: Quarrier Press, 2003).

Hatfield, Elliot G. *The Hatfields.* Revised and edited by Leonard Roberts and Henry P. Scalf. (Pikeville, Kentucky: The Big Sandy Valley Historical Society, 1988).

Hewett, J.B. *Roster of Union Soldiers, 1861-1865.* Vol. 18, Kentucky and Tennessee. (Wilmington, NC: Broadfoot Publishing, 2000).

Hill, Jeffrey A. *The 26th Ohio Veteran Volunteer Infantry: The Groundhog Regiment.* (Bloomington, IN: Author House Publishing, 2010).

Jones, Virgil Carrington. *The Hatfields and the McCoys.* (Chapel Hill, NC: University of North Carolina Press, 1948, First Ed.).

King, Dean. *The Hatfields and McCoys: The True Story.* (New York: Back Bay Books, 2013).

Linger, James C. *Confederate Military Organizations in West Virginia 1861-1865*. 8th Edition. (Tulsa OK: Privately published monograph, 2004).

Lowry, Terry. *The Battle of Scary Creek.* (Charleston, West Virginia: Quarrier Press, 1986).

_____. *22nd Virginia Infantry*. (Lynchburg, Virginia: H.E. Howard, 1988).

McCoy, Truda Williams. *The McCoys: Their Story as told to the Author by Eyewitnesses and Descendants*. (Pikeville, Kentucky: Preservation Council Press of Pike County, 2000).

Moore, Frank (Ed.). *The Rebellion Record: A Diary of American Events, with Documents, Narratives, Illustrative Incidents, Poetry, Etc.* Vol. 3. (New York: G.P. Putnam, 1862).

Morgan, John. *The Last Dollar*. (Original printing 1909; St. Albans, West Virginia: St. Albans Historical Society, Reprinted 2012).

John E. Pearce. *Days of Darkness: The Feuds of Eastern Kentucky*. (Lexington, KY: University of Kentucky Press, 1994).

Prichard, James M. *The Devil At Large: Devil Anse's War.* In William Davis. *Virginia at War*, 1863. (Lexington, KY: University of Kentucky Press, 2008).

Osborne, R. and Jeffrey C. Weaver. *The Virginia State Rangers and Virginia State Line*. (Lynchburg, VA: H.E. Howard, 1994).

Rice, Otis R. *The Hatfields and McCoys.* (Lexington, Kentucky: University Press of Kentucky, 2010).

Spears, John. *The Dramatic Story of a Mountain Feud*, Annotated Edition. (Charleston, South Carolina: Createspace.com, 2015, Originally published 1888).

Scott, James L. *36th Virginia Infantry*. (Lynchburg, Virginia: H.E. Howard, 2nd. Ed., 1987).

Snuff, Stephen W. *The Blood Feud: Devil Anse Hatfield and The Real McCoys*. (British Columbia: Trufford Publishing, 2012).

Sutherland, Jasper E. *Pioneer Recollections of Southern West Virginia. (Clintwood, West Virginia: Mullins Printing*, Originally published October 1862, reprinted 1984).

Thomas, Jean. *Big Sandy*. (New York: Henry Holt & Co., 1940).

Thompson, Robert M. *Twelve Pole Terror: The Legend of Rebel Bill Smith.* (Wayne, WV: R.M. Thompson Books, 2015).

_____. *Pioneers, Rebels & Wolves: A History of Wayne County.* (Wayne, WV: R.M. Thompson Books, 2010).

Wallace, Lee A. A Guide to Virginia Military Organizations 1861-1865. (Lynchburg, Virginia: H.E. Howard, 1986).

Waller, Altina. *Hatfields, McCoys and Social Change in Appalachia 1860-1900.* (Chapel Hill, NC: University of North Carolina Press, 1988).

Weaver, Jeffrey C. *45th Battalion Virginia Infantry, Smith & Count's Battalions of Partisan Rangers.* (Lynchburg, Virginia: H.E. Howard, 1994).

Manuscripts

Alexander Messer Papers. Charles Allen Reed Collection, Civil War Manuscripts, MS2012-011. WV State Archives.

Dan Cunningham. "Murders in Jackson and Roane Counties, West Virginia." (1931) Manuscripts Collection, No. 364.152 C973, WV State Archives (1931).

Logan County Wildcats, Logbook, 1830-1900. Accession No. 1977/11.0206 (MS-59) Marshall University Special Collections (MUSC), Marshall University Library, Huntington, WV.

Micajah Woods Papers 1847-1926. Alderman Library Special Collections, Manuscripts, CN 10279, University of Virginia Library, Charlottesville, Virginia.

Seth A. Nichols. "Let Us Bury and Forget: Civil War Memory and Identity in Cabell County, West Virginia, 1865-1915." 2016. Unpublished Thesis, Marshall University Department of History, 1-12; 14-22; 27-39; Theses, Dissertations and Capstones. 1066. http://mds.marshall.edu/etd/1066.

Bibliography

Government Archival Sources

Arthur I. Boreman Papers (1823-1896). West Virginia & Regional History Center, Call No. A&M 0104. West Virginia University Library, Morgantown, West Virginia.

Camp Chase Paroles, 1862-1865. Series 1543, Ohio Historical Society, Columbus Ohio.

Code of Virginia. Second Edition. Including Legislation to the Year 1860 (Richmond: Ritchie, Dunnavant & Co., 1860).

Compiled Service Records, Record Groups 94, 109, M319, M324, M397, M861, National Archives.

Department of Confederate Military Records, Accession No. 27684, Series 2, Unit, Militia & State Line Records, Subseries 2, 7 & 8. Library of Virginia, Richmond, Virginia.

Journal of the Virginia House of Delegates, 1857-1858, SB73, SB395 and SB493. (Richmond, VA: William F. Ritchie, Public Printer, 1857-1858).

Journal of the Virginia House of Delegates, 1859-1860. SB500. (Richmond, VA: William F. Ritchie, Public Printer, 1857-1858).

Journal of the Senate of the Commonwealth of Virginia, General Assembly. Bill No. 119. (Richmond, Virginia: J.E. Goode, Publisher, 1861).

Kentucky Department of Libraries and Archives (KYDA).

Medical Descriptive List, U.S. Army General Hospital, Lexington, Kentucky, Vol. 13(1), Kentucky Department of Libraries and Archives, Frankfort, Kentucky.

Muster Rolls of Paroled and Exchanged Confederate Prisoners of War, 1861-1865, RG 109, Identifier No. 652414, Inventory No. PI101, National Archives.

U.S. War Department, *The War of the Rebellion: A Compilation of the Official Records of the Union and Confederate Armies, 128 Vols.* (Washington, DC: Government Printing Office, 1881-1901).

Pike County Kentucky Tax Assessment Book (1861), and Pike County Civil Cases No.'s 2377 and 2373.

Records of the Colonial Militia through World War I. Ca. 1936, MS80-22, WV State Archives.

Records of Confederate Prisoners of War, 1861-1865, RG 109, M598, National Archives.

Records of the Adjutant and Inspector General's Department. Records relating to Courts-Martial, 1861-65, RG 109, M836, National Archives.

Report of the Adjutant General of the State of Kentucky. Vol. 2 1861-1866. (Frankfurt, Kentucky: John H. Harney, Public Printer, 1867).

1830, 1840, 1850 and 1860 United States Census and Slave Schedules. Record Group 29, Microfilm 19, 653, & 1358, 91. 1860: 289, Logan County, Va., June 1, 1860, Enumerated by B.S. Chapman. Washington, D.C.: National Archives and Records Administration.

West Virginia Adjutant General Papers, Union Militia, 1861-1865, AR-373, WV State Archives.

West Virginia Adjutant General Papers, Pierpont-Samuels Collection, AR1722, WV State Archives.

Periodicals

David Behar. "Flashbacks and Posttraumatic Stress Symptoms among Combat Veterans." *Comprehensive Psychiatry*, Vol. 28(6), (Nov.-Dec. 1987), 459-466.

Guthrie, Charles S. Review of The McCoys. *Kentucky Folklore Record: Bowling Green*. Vol. 23(2), (1977): 53.

Harris, F.S. "Noted Character of West Virginia." *Confederate Veteran,* (October 1900): 205-206.

C.W. Hoge, et. Al. "Combat Duty in Iraq and Afghanistan: Mental Health Problems and Barriers to Care." New England Journal of Medicine, Vol. 351(1), (July 1, 2004), 13-22.

Hyer, L., Summers, M. N., Braswell, L., & Boyd, S. "Posttraumatic stress disorder: Silent problem among older combat veterans." *Psychotherapy: Theory, Research, Practice, Training, 32*(2), (1995), 348–364.

Ludwell H. Johnson (Ed.). "The Horrible Butcheries of West Virginia: Dan Cunningham on the Hatfield-McCoy Feud: Ans' Hatfield War History." *West Virginia History,* Vol. 46, 1985-1986, 42.

T.N. Sayer et al. "Reintegration Problems and Treatment Interests Among Iraq and Afghanistan Combat Veterans Receiving VA Medical Care." *Psychiatric Services*, Vol. 61(6), (June 2010), 589-597.

R.E. Strange and D.E. Brown, Jr. "Home from the War: A Study of Psychiatric Problems in Vietnam Returnees." *American Journal of Psychiatry*, Vol. 127(4), (Oct. 1970), 488-492.

T. Yager, R. Laufer & M. Gallops. "Problems Associated with War Experience in Men of the Vietnam Generation." Archive of General Psychiatry, Vol. 41(4), (1984), 327-333.

Newspapers

"Devil Anse Tells How." *Bluefield Daily Telegraph,* October 22, 1920. Newspapers on Microfilm, Misc. Rolls, WV State Archives.

"From Capt. Shaw's Company." *Bucyrus Journal*, October 18, 1861. Letter written by Charles A. Stough, October 7th, 1861 at Camp Piatt. Civil War and Statehood Timeline: September 25, 1861. Online: www.wvculture.org/history/sesquicentennial.

"A Splendid Achievement of the Ohio Zouaves – 'Wood Up' the Battle Cry." *Chicago Daily Tribune*, October 9, 1861. Transcribed by Brandon R. Kirk at http://brandonraykirk.com.

Cincinnati Commercial. October 3, 1861: www.wvculture.org/history/sesquicentennial; "The Situation." *National Republican,* October 7, 1861. Transcribed by Brandon R. Kirk: http://brandonraykirk.com.

"A Confederate Camp in Western Virginia Broken Up and Routed." Cleveland Morning Leader, September 6 & 12, 1861. Transcribed by Brandon R. Kirk at http://brandonraykirk.com.

Evening Star (Washington, DC), October 4, 1861.Transcribed by Brandon R. Kirk at http://brandonraykirk.com.

"Floyd Woman's Memories Breathe Life into Legend." *Floyd County Times* May 18, 1988," Vol. 51(20), 1. *Floyd County History Collection*, accessed December 10, 2019. http://history.fclib.org/items/show/2869.

"Details of the Boone Court House Fight." *Gallipolis Journal*, September 12, 1861. Vol. 26(43). Chronicling America, Library of Congress. www.chroniclingamerica.loc.gov.

"Spurlock Caught!" *Gallipolis Journal*, February 18, 1864. Vol. 29(13). Chronicling America, Library of Congress. www.chroniclingamerica.loc.gov.

"Fights in Wayne Co., Va." *The Ironton Register*, August 29, 1861, Vol. 11(38) & "Narrow Escapes." *The Ironton Register*, April 5, 1888. Newspaper and Periodical Reading Room, LCCN: 84028882, Library of Congress, Washington, D.C.

Logan Banner, December 2, 1938. Newspapers on Microfilm, Misc. Rolls, WV State Archives.

Logan Democrat newspaper, September 19, 1912 and October 26, 1911. Brandon R. Kirk Blog. Online: www.brandonraykirk.com.

"Time-Dimmed Record of Early Logan County Families in 1852-1877 Period in Old Books Found at Pecks Mill." *Logan Telegraph*. November 3, 1936. Newspapers on Microfilm, Logan Banner, Misc. Reels, M-6. WV State Archives.

Louisville Daily Journal, November 12, 1864, Vol. 33(2). Newspapers and Periodicals Reading Room, SN: 84027471, Library of Congress, Washington, D.C.

Lynchburg Virginian. October 24, 1862. Serial & Government Publications Division, Call No. SN-84024646, Newspaper & Current Periodical Reading Room (Madison LM133). Library of Congress.

National Republican, October 7, 1861; Transcribed by Brandon R. Kirk at http://brandonraykirk.com.

Star of the Kanawha Valley, Buffalo, Va. Newspapers on Microfilm: Misc. Reels, M-16, 54, 57, 126. WV State Archives.

Staunton Spectator, September 25, 1861; Transcribed by Brandon R. Kirk at http://brandonraykirk.com.

"*Wayne Court House Taken.*" *New York Times*, September 15, 1861. www.nytimes.archives.

"Boone Court House, Va." *Richmond Daily Dispatch*, September 6, 1861, Vol. 20(55). Library of Congress: www.chroniclingamerican.loc.gov.

Sandy Valley Advocate, Ca*tlettsburg (Ky.) Advocate*, August 28, 1861. University of Kentucky Archives: www.uky.edu/Libraries/NDNP/listcivilwar.

"Devil Anse tells the true history of the famous Hatfield-McCoy Feud." *Wheeling Intelligencer,* November 23, 1889, Vol. 78(39). Library of Congress:www.chroniclingamerica.loc.gov.

Websites & Blogs

Ancestry.com. *West Virginia, Deaths Index, 1853-1973* [database on-line]. Provo, UT, USA: Ancestry.com Operations, Inc., 2011.

Brandon R. Kirk Blog. Summary of Article posted online March 4, 2019: https://brandonraykirk.com/tag/joseph-hinchman/.

Timeline of West Virginia: Civil War and Statehood, September 1, 1861. www.wvculture.org.

United States Census, 1860. Database with images. *Family Search.* http://FamilySearch.org: 21 March 2020. From "1860 U.S. Federal Census - Population." Database. *Fold3.com.* http://www.fold3.com. Citing NARA microfilm publication M653. Washington, D.C.: National Archives and Records Administration, n.d.

1860 U.S. Census; https://www.geni.com/people/Randolph-Randall-McCoy: see notes by Maria Edmonds-Zediker, Volunteer Curator, June 16, 2019; Ancestry.com. *Kentucky, County Marriage Records, 1783-1965* [database on-line]. Lehi, UT, USA: Ancestry.com Operations, Inc., 2016.

Yates Publishing. *U.S. and International Marriage Records, 1560-1900* [database on-line]. Provo, UT, USA: Ancestry.com Operations Inc, 2004.

West Virginia, Births Index, 1804-1938 [database on-line]. Provo, UT, USA: Ancestry.com Operations, Inc., 2011.

Legal and Public Documents

Pike County Kentucky Circuit Court Cases No. 2155, 2177, 2355, 2386, and 2774.

Personal Communications

Email: April 3, 2020. Mary Hinchman, Hinchman Historical Society, Lexington, Kentucky.

Name Index

About the Author

Philip Hatfield, PhD., is a native West Virginian with family roots in the Logan and Mingo County areas. He holds a bachelor's degree in psychology and history, two master's degrees in psychology, and a doctorate in Clinical Psychology. He has written five books and numerous scholarly articles on the Civil War and is a member of the Company of Military Historians. Dr. Hatfield is also the great-great-great grandson of Alexander (Alec, Ale) Hatfield, a cousin of Devil Anse Hatfield. Alec Hatfield, who was from Pike County, Kentucky, served in the 12th Kentucky Infantry (US), 1861-1865, and participated in Major General William T. Sherman's famous march through Georgia and the Carolinas.

35th Star Publishing
Charleston, West Virginia
www.35thstar.com

Made in the USA
Columbia, SC
26 July 2021